# An Interdisciplinary Introduction to Women's Studies

Edited by Brianne Friel & Robert L. Giron

Montgomery College

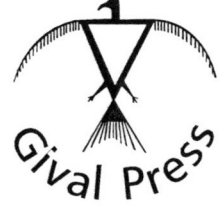

Arlington, Virginia

Copyright © 2005 by Gival Press, LLC.

All rights reserved under International and Pan-American Copyright Conventions. Printed in the United States of America.

With the exception of brief quotations in the body of critical articles or reviews, no part of this book may be reproduced or transmitted in any form or by any means, graphic, electronic, or mechanical, including photocopying, recording, taping, or by any information storage or retrieval system, without the permission in writing from the publisher.

Published by Gival Press, an imprint of Gival Press, LLC.

For information please write:

Gival Press, LLC, P. O. Box 3812, Arlington, VA 22203.

Website: *www.givalpress.com*

Email: givalpress@yahoo.com

First edition ISBN 1-928589-29-4

Library of Congress Control Number: 2005921153

Format and design by Ken Schellenberg.

# Contents

*Introduction*
    by Brianne Friel ................................................................. 7

*Global Women's Studies: An Essay in Three Life-Stories*
    by Rita S. Kranidis ........................................................... 15

*Cuban Women: Betrayed by Revolution*
    by Teresa Bevin ............................................................... 24

*Women's Work:*
*Environmental Activism in India and Kenya*
    by Dianne Ganz Scheper ................................................. 37

*Where Are the Women in Women's Health?*
    by Maureen Edwards ..................................................... 58

*Caught Between Homophobia and Peer Pressure:*
*A Classroom Experiment*
    by Teresa Bevin ............................................................... 74

*Women in Front of and Behind the Camera*
    by Robert L. Giron .......................................................... 83

*Their Eyes Were Watching God:*
*Subversive Quest for A Woman's Voice*
    by Brianne Friel ............................................................. 99

*Giving Voice to the Unspeakable:*
*Contemporary Poems by Women*
    by Kay Bosgraaf ........................................................... 114

*Women in Philosophy*
    by Tülin M. Levitas ...................................................... 131

Contributors ........................................................................ 143

# Introduction

## by Brianne Friel

When I was coordinator of the Women's Studies Program at Montgomery College, people often would ask me, "Is women's studies really still necessary?" Or, a variation on the same question, "If women's studies really is successful, then, won't it become obsolete?" Behind the questions might have been a general sense of confusion as to what really goes on in the women's studies classroom, a much-mythologized but often little-understood curriculum.

These questions are answered beautifully in this collection, written entirely by faculty of the Women's Studies Program at Montgomery College. Because women's studies is interdisciplinary, running through traditional disciplines such as English, history, and philosophy, as well as newer ones such as film and health studies, the answer to the question "What is women's studies?" is best answered through the disciplines. It is a way of thinking about a field, such as literature or politics, with a mind to where the women have been and how they have been treated, so that the way one approaches that subject will never again be the same. This is the way that Tülin Levitas, author of the essay "Women in Philosophy," approached her field when she wondered why, as a graduate student in philosophy, she was taught about no women philosophers, and went off in search of those women who surely thought and wrote about philosophy through the ages. It is the way that Teresa Bevin approaches world history in her essay "Cuban Women: Betrayed by Revolution" when she documents how Fidel Castro's revolution has left women behind, breaking up families, social and religious networks, and forcing many women into prostitution. In "Women in Front of and Behind the Camera," Robert L. Giron looks for women in film, and finds, behind the perplexing combination of misogyny, violence against women, and fetishism of the female form, a fear of the woman's innate physical power, an attempt to render her less potent (to castrate, if there were such a word for trying to strip a woman of her vital female power) either by isolating and exaggerating her features to bring her power under male control, or by making her more masculine so that she can be dealt with as an equal.

Kay Bosgraaf illustrates the kind of thinking that typifies feminist theory in her essay "Giving Voice to the Unspeakable: Contemporary Poems by Women." Contemporary women poets are "revising what is seen and heard…making the invisible visible, the hidden revealed, and the silenced heard." They "actively question what has been left behind in the margins." The poem that Bosgraaf refers to, Maxine Kumin's "Photograph, Maryland Agricultural College Livestock Show, 1924," describes a picture of white college boys photographed with their prize-winning cow, while the black farm workers stand just outside the camera's lens. Women's studies has come to look for the "marginalized," that is, not to accept what the lens has focused on as the only picture, the only story, but to look as well for what is behind the scene.

Because academic women's studies looks behind the scenes for other stories, it ends up offering some alternate ways of thinking about beliefs or concepts once taken for granted. Bosgraaf suggests that women poets have, in fact, challenged the unspoken values of poets that favored *intellectualizing* an event over *experiencing* it, so that writing is a way of experiencing more keenly rather than a method to catalogue experience. In this way, Bosgraaf argues, women have redefined what is "intellectual" or "intelligent" as not only what is ordered and analyzed but also what is experienced and felt, so that, as Bosgraaf quotes poet Rorie Graham, "thinking deeply is feeling deeply. They're interchangeable." In much the same fashion, Dianne Ganz Scheper causes us to reverse our thinking of the meaning of the words "progress" and "development": if so-called progress is depleting our earth's resources, then, is it really progress? If so-called development is destroying the landscape and depriving us of clean air, water, and food, then is it really development, or is it destruction?

Women's contributions have begun to reinvigorate, or re-form, the content of the disciplines. This is the case of women who are writing and publishing poems that are transforming what is considered serious enough for that genre, as Kay Bosgraaf describes in her essay: "As these writers create their own rules for writing poetry, they free themselves to write about new subjects such as female forebears, mother-child relationships, child sexual abuse, and clinical depression, amongst others." One of the important by-products of academic feminism is that subjects, such as these, that are integral to women's lives, now can be considered and taken seriously; in poetry, now, "the personal experience of women, formerly considered too personal, private, unimportant, or shameful for poetry, has now very often become its subject and theme." Robert L. Giron sees in contemporary women filmmakers a shared interest in the struggles of all people, hence he sees them contributing to film the "social and political means to bring these issues to the attention of the majority who do not have to endure hardships such as discrimination, racism, sexism, and ... atrocities done to humanity in the name of advancement of one's culture, political agenda, or greed."

Women's studies recovers for history the contributions of women that have been ignored or undervalued. Levitas wonders how the history of the Western world might have differed had women philosophers, such as Héloïse, the 12$^{th}$ century philosopher, been more influential: whereas "the conceptual framework of Western metaphysics has been created on...dichotomies [body/soul, woman/man; black/white], which have been used to justify racism, sexism, and repression in general when different groups of people have been characterized as the 'other'," Héloïse "refused to accept these dualistic views, as becomes evident in her concept of disinterested love and morality of intent. Thus her contribution to the history of philosophy is a more holistic view of human nature and a more responsible concept of love." And the ancient philosopher Aesara, 350 years before the Christian era, believed that "all moral action, whether it involves the individual, the family, or society at large, needs to reflect the appropriate proportions of rationality, compassion, and will power"; her "emphasis on love and compassion as necessary conditions for moral action constitutes Aesara's important contribution to the history of philosophy." Levitas also reveals to her readers the women philosophers who, "even as recently as the 19$^{th}$ century...did not dare publish their works under their own names. Instead, they had to publish under their male colleagues' names." For example,

> all of Harriet Taylor's philosophic work was published under John Stuart Mill's name, and Anna Doyle Wheeler's work, *The Appeal of One Half of the Human Race, Women Against the Pretensions of the Other Half, Men, to Restrain Them in Political and Thence in Civil and Domestic Slavery* (1825), was published under William Thompson's name. Both Mill and Thompson credit Taylor and Wheeler with the content of their works, but nevertheless the publications did not carry their names as their rightful authors.

Women's studies also analyzes women's living conditions and how these have influenced their work. Dianne Ganz Scheper's essay "Women's Work: Environmental Activism in India and Kenya" explains why women, who are the primary gatherers of food and water over most of the earth, have been most moved to protest depletion of natural resources, and how they have had to join forces with other women in similar situations to work against the large corporations who seek to profit by "developing" their land. Women's studies investigates the ways that women have worked around discrimination to contribute to their fields, as I do in my essay "The Subversive Quest for Voice in Zora Neale Hurston's *Their Eyes Were Watching God*," showing how Hurston, like many women writers before her, had to use keen rhetorical strategy in order to be published in a sexist, racist society.

What we learn from women's studies can save our lives. In Maureen Edwards' essay "Where are the Women in Women's Health?" she discusses the appalling paucity of women included in medical research, an omission that costs women's lives. As Edwards explains, a 1995 Gallup poll confirmed that one out of three physicians was unaware that heart attacks are the number one killer of women as well as men. So women die twice as much as men do following a first heart attack. Another major killer of women is, unbelievably, domestic violence. As Edwards states, "violence has recently been identified by public health officials as a major public health issue affecting both the physical and emotional health of women and children... Domestic violence injures or kills thousands of women each year." In this environment which fails in some measure to support women either socially, medically, or through the media, Edwards exhorts her students, "If you do not seek to educate yourself on the issues, don't be surprised if society doesn't either. Societal change begins with individual commitment. Each and every woman should and must be an advocate for her own health." Dianne Ganz Scheper's essay also shows how women's increasing influence can save our lives by reframing the thinking that favors commodity production over the health and life of our natural resources. According to Scheper, ecofeminists envision instead "an economically and ecologically sustainable future...based on harmonious, non-exploitative relationships between human beings and between people and nature," a future that will sustain us all.

We need Women's studies because we should know about women who are still very much oppressed by society. In Rita Kranidis's essay "Global Women's Studies: An Essay in Three Lives," we learn about "women in India who are burned alive because they are not deemed economically or socially desirable," and of "women who are subjected to ritual genital mutilation to ensure their value in the marriage market." We need women's studies because, as Bevin reports, websites that traffic in women—a practice, for practical purposes, akin to slavery—are sponsored by the Cuban government and because, as she further points out, there are similar internet sites in the Philippines, Russia, and Thailand. We need women's studies because, as Kranidis reveals, the three women closest to her in her family all have been affected by rape and domestic violence. We need to know these things because, as Kranidis insists, this "is where the truth lies," and because knowing the truth overcomes dangerous myths such as "things were/are not so bad," that "that was then, this is now," that "that would not happen here," and, finally, that "one or two extreme examples are not representative of reality." In our world, we cannot afford to gloss over women's oppression, or the oppression of any group around the world, because, ultimately, what affects one woman—indeed, what affects one *person* of either gender—affects us all. As Kranidis articulates, the same system that terrorized Iraqi women crossed our borders to terrorize us. Scheper calls the so-called "third-world" women fighting for their lands "the proverbial canaries in the coal mines" who show us "the early and devastating human effects of environmental degradation" that will affect us all. Women's lives, women's voices, have a lot to teach us, except that "as a society, we have not been listening very closely or empathetically," as Kranidis points out. And, anyway, why ignore, and so waste, the valuable insight and experience of more than one half the population, from all history?

Moreover, feminism increasingly concerns itself not only with women, but also with prejudice in general, with ways that society seeks to limit any group of people. What we've learned from women's struggles can be applied to groups that find themselves out of favor because of race, class, sexual orientation, or whatever factor society arbitrarily selects. Teresa Bevin, a sociologist and women's studies professor, explores this theme in her essay "Caught Between Homophobia and Peer Pressure: A Classroom Experiment," where she discovers that peer pressure is influential in keeping her students from expressing their true opinion regarding a population.

We need women's studies because it can set an example for what women, even seemingly powerless ones, can do. As Scheper describes, women in developing nations "are demonstrating how, even against heavy odds, women can join together to defend the integrity of their homelands and the dignity of their way of life.... In cultures where women traditionally have no political power, these women are discovering the value of the crucial problems facing the world today" and teaching us "that problems which often look intractable can be confronted by individuals or small groups acting together and mobilizing others for the common good."

The disciplines represented in this collection are by no means comprehensive; no attempt was made to cover with any completeness the number of disciplines to which feminist theory can be applied, since this is virtually limitless, and no pretense at "mastery" or completeness of any topic is made. Since academic feminism is still a relatively new field, teachers and students of women's studies are comfortable experimenting, trying new things, failing at some, and stretching ourselves. Because we invite diversity into our curriculum, we become comfortable with difference, and yet, we see shared components to what we study, whether it be a classic work or the voice of a working-class woman. As Rita Kranidis says in her essay, "We can speak from a place that is authentically ours but can be shared by all. We can initiate a kind of discourse that is already waiting for articulation... [a] new discourse of women's studies [that is] global in its perspective, encompassing a number of different languages and customs. We would have to learn and study continuously because we would need to always traverse oceans and realities to reach a greater understanding." And, perhaps it is obvious, yet too often overlooked, that this understanding must extend to the men with whom we share our lives and the globe, for, in these times that are dangerous in so many ways, we need to call on men as our allies, to teach and set an example to young men and boys that "real" men don't abuse, mistreat, or exploit women. As Robert L. Giron, an important contributor to the Women's Studies Program at Montgomery College, says in his essay "Women in Front of and Behind the Camera," men can be feminist critics—and women are not necessarily feminist—and men should be encouraged to join the women's studies classroom and, thankfully, are doing so. Men enrolled in women's studies classes at Montgomery College have valued the experience and found that the mostly-exaggerated "male bashing" was not a reality.

We hope that reading this book will be like visiting the campus and dipping into a few classes, a few minutes in a Literature by Women class, a few minutes in Women's History or Women's Health, and so on. And, we hope that you like what you see enough to pursue more classes in women's studies.

The editors of this book would like to thank, first of all, the women's studies faculty members who generously contributed their valuable expertise, time, and goodwill by writing essays for this book. They are dedicated and busy teachers at Montgomery College, and taking the time to document a small portion of their accumulated knowledge is no small feat. We would like to thank the current director of the Women's Studies Program at Montgomery College, Genevieve Carminati, for giving us her blessing and supporting us 100 percent in the endeavor, and we would like to thank Carolyn Terry, the dean in charge of women's studies, Mary Kay Shartle-Galotto and Judy Ackerman, the provosts who have been in term since the book's inception, for their moral and practical support, and Paula D. Matuskey, the humanities dean at Takoma Park, for helping to create a women's studies program on the campus. These Montgomery College administrators are models of supportive managers, since they stand at the ready to do what they can to release their faculty to fulfill their goals and make their dreams come true. There has never been a time that we have come to these administrators with an idea, a request, or a goal that they have not taken their own time and initiative to help us make it come true. Significantly, we would like to thank Dr. Charlene Nunley, a great woman college president who attends each and every scholarship breakfast to sit with and encourage the students with stories of her own educational journey, and who takes a personal interest in every course and event of the women's studies program. It is this kind of support that makes a program happen and then keeps it running. Finally, we would like to thank the students of Montgomery College. They are the reason we keep coming back year after year, the ones who inspire us to try a little harder, to work a little longer on a special project or event, or a new class lesson. Our students have amazing stories. Many have come a great distance, either literally or figuratively, to attain their education at Montgomery College. They love education for education's sake, and they teach us all about strength, tenacity, and courage every day. To all the students, faculty, staff, and administrators at Montgomery College who work so beautifully together as a team and have made the women's studies program one of the best in the country, we thank you.

# Global Women's Studies: An Essay in Three Life-Stories

by Rita S. Kranidis

Growing up in Greece during the 1960s, I observed very closely the lives of the women who figured prominently in my life. My personal investment in Women's Studies stems from their stories, and so I will share a few of them here.

## Paraskevi

She was not very attractive and a bit clumsy, socially, but she smiled easily and was very kind. She stopped going to school after the sixth grade, as was common; her grades were acceptable but not remarkable. She was a village girl who worked on the farm with the rest of her family, digging, irrigating, and picking fruit. The harvest of this work sustained them for the whole year. She did her work well—better than most, even. She worked tirelessly, as if her body enjoyed the physical activity and the exhaustion that followed. On Sundays, she wore her only dress and accompanied her mother and sisters to church.

When she became 20 years old, it was decided that she would marry. Nothing was said about it. There was no need. The village was a small one, and everyone knew the young women who were of age. One of the families in town approached her parents, and then they told her. Paraskevi accepted the arrangement because the young man seemed good enough to her, and she had had no other offers. The danger lay in not accepting a proposal and then becoming an old maid. She could not risk that. In the small village, there would be no place for her whatsoever. She accepted the proposal, and was then engaged, in the traditional custom. Both families met at her parents' house, where a dinner was served and agreements on a dowry made. The mood was celebratory, festive, an atmosphere of relief—but Paraskevi seemed unhappy. She would soon tell her mother that she had made a mistake. Her fiancée was unkind and unpredictable. She did not want to marry him. She said this, reluctantly, even though she knew that it was not acceptable for a woman to break an engagement. She would be branded as an impure woman and eventually marry with difficulty, if at all. There was no place for unmarried women in her village.

Despite her protests and tears, her uncharacteristically strong words ("whatever comes of this will be on your heads; I would be marrying him unwillingly"), and her withdrawal from her sisters and friends, the wedding took place as planned. Her marriage proved more difficult than anyone had imagined. The shutters of her house, built by her parents on the edge of town as part of her dowry, were often closed. She did not go out much, so that her mother and sisters took turns visiting to find out how she was. She stood in the door, the house dark behind her. She said she was okay. It was not until months later that she confided the truth to her mother: her husband was beating her.

No one intervened. Her situation did not change, but she was changed. She withdrew and kept to herself. She cried sometimes, but mainly she looked off into the distance. As time went on, she had less and less to say. When they took her to the city by ferry, to see a psychiatrist, she jumped into the water 20 feet below. She had meant to escape but was pulled out and delivered to the doctor, who prescribed many medications. She has taken these medications for the last 30 years. Her husband has changed very little, and she has a mentally retarded daughter to whom she is devoted. She has few interactions with her family and no close friends in the village.

## Sevasti

She had always been told she was not a "real" daughter because her mother, a widow at 22, had remarried—she was an outsider. Her brothers and sisters loved her, but her stepfather made it clear that she was not his own. He expected gratitude for keeping this woman's child in his home, among his own children. She was expected to work harder, to be more meek and obedient, and to draw as little attention to herself as possible.

She wanted to stay in school and her teachers encouraged this since she was intelligent, but her father said he could not spare her from the farm. She was also needed at home, to care for the younger children and the housework. When she gave up on her dream of getting an education, her greater worry was that she would not be given a dowry. Her stepfather had made it clear that she could expect very little. Who would want to marry her? The village people thought of her as a good girl but unlucky. They could not have their sons marry for nothing.

Despite all this, she made every effort to assert herself. She refused offers of marriage to the various men who were interested in her. Her stepfather, eager to be rid of her, paid a local man to rape her. That way she would lose her status in the world's eyes and could be forced to marry anyone willing to have her. She fought off the rapist and ran home, but knew from that point on that she must marry or leave soon. She need not have worried too much, however, because she stood out from the other young women in the village. Her father had been from a different region and so her features were distinct. She was also intelligent and not frivolous. An outsider, a man who visited the village one day, noticed her from a distance. He had just come back from Belgium, where he had been working for some years. He was a plumber and could make a good living, and he seemed to be kind. He did not insist on a dowry— it was hardly "democratic," he said. He was radical. He asked to marry her and she accepted. They left to live in the city and moved to New York many years later.

## Popi

She was a dreamer. She grew up dreaming of meeting a handsome man who would marry her, like the ones she saw in films. She went to the movies every Sunday, sometimes with her brother, as was customary, and sometimes with a girlfriend or two. She was one of two children, much spoiled by her mother. They lived comfortably. She enjoyed the newest fashions and had new dresses made more regularly than other young women. She did not go to school beyond the sixth grade because she was not interested in studies, but enjoyed socializing with friends and neighbors. She read magazines, listened to soap operas on the radio, and polished her nails.

The man she had waited for came one day. He was handsome, very charming, and on his way to finishing at a technical school, which would allow him to make a good living. They talked now and again, casually, as neighbors, when it became clear that he was interested in her as well. She waited for him while he went to Italy to improve his craft, and then again when he went to the capitol to apprentice. Eventually, they married. Soon after the wedding, however, he became violent toward her, never for any reason. He demanded that she not go out and became increasingly rigid. She was commonly seen with bruises on her arms or on her face. She wore scarves and sunglasses to cover up the marks, and wore long sleeves even during the long summers. She denied that her husband beat her and simply said, "this does not concern you; you must not interfere in my marriage." Nonetheless, sometimes the neighbors would call the police when her screams pierced the peace of the afternoon siesta. When the police came, she defended her husband, and so they left.

Thirty years later, Popi lives with her husband. Her two sons are grown and married. They do not talk to their father and only infrequently to Popi.

The three women whose stories I have shared here are my mother's sister, my mother, and my uncle's wife. I saw the drama of their lives played out over many years, and learned from their personal tragedies. They taught me that the lives of women are a very different lot from the lives of men and that I had to be very careful about the choices I made. However, it was not until I took a women's studies class in college that I was able to process these stories within a social and historical context and to appreciate their importance for my own life choices. They lay dormant, waiting for me to acknowledge them, to make some space in my mind and consciousness that would allow them to surface as the monumental events they were. It was not until I began to analyze women's lives on a broader scale that these stories came together in my mind as the reality that provided my foundations as a woman and as a scholar. Today, it is important for me to remember them not only for my own benefit but also for that of my students—and to offer their lives as a stark reminder that what we do to improve the life of one woman will most likely reverberate over time.

And so this narrative continues. When I returned to Greece in 1984, I realized that I was no longer a Greek young woman (who ought to be thinking about getting married) but someone else—different rules applied to me and my life now; I had new options. I had graduated from college and soon would be starting graduate school. During this visit, I heard a word with which I was not familiar: *isotita*. As generally happens with immigrants, my long absence from my country had created gaps in understanding and communication. This word was not in my vocabulary, but I was to learn that it meant *equality*, and that it was being used specifically to talk about relations between men and women. I was surprised. I heard village women engage this word in conversations openly and even defiantly, sometimes in friendly banter with their husbands.

What had happened to bring about this change? What had caused one of my aunts, still living in a small, remote village, to say with confidence, "Of course women must have *isotita*"? There was a new understanding about women's roles, one to which I was not privy. I learned that issues of women's rights were in the public domain now, since the Prime Minister's wife, a non-Greek, had initiated this discourse by speaking openly about her concerns for Greek women. This sudden transformation had been triggered by one person! I was filled with optimism for the future of all women, everywhere.

It would have been tidier politically, for the change to have come from a Greek woman, but that was not how it happened. In discussions of women's rights today, some will generally caution that we must be careful not to tread on other cultures, not to impose our Western ways on the world. This argument is disingenuous. It assumes that all native women are fully compliant with the means of their own oppression, when in fact —as ever so many stories demonstrate— we know that is not the case. It also assumes that women from industrialized nations are the only ones putting forth arguments for women's empowerment. Voices of resistance have arisen from women in virtually all cultures for countless generations. Trinh Minh-Ha (Vietnam), Nawal El Sadawii (Egypt), Mahasweta Devi (India), Mariama Ba (Senegal), Lorna Goodison (Jamaica), among so many other writers and scholars, have been telling us for some time that they stand opposed to those forces in their cultures that oppress women. Those who are genuinely interested in the lives and wishes of women all over the globe will discover an impressive body of scholarship on international women's issues.[1] However, the fault seems to lie in that as a society, we have not been listening very closely or empathetically. If the women who are systematically oppressed, traded, and mutilated were elephants or tigers, the world would have taken swift action long ago. The human rights of women have not always been viewed as inalienable and, historically, there has been a general reluctance to take up the subject of women, who are viewed as the property of men.

As the globe becomes an increasingly smaller place, we can no longer maintain false cultural boundaries of noninterference when it comes to gender while renegotiating those boundaries in every other respect. Nations are beginning to understand that some women need to be protected from the threats of their own cultures and countries. As a first step in the right direction, many now unconditionally grant political asylum to African women escaping ritual genital mutilation. The time has come to look at individual women's lives again, with the conviction that they matter a great deal. Their life narratives must proliferate in our classrooms, in our research and in our academic conversations. Every story that finds a voice among us represents hundreds of thousands of others that will not be heard. As the cultural critic Trinh Minh-ha has elaborated, as scholars and teachers, we participate in the time-honored tradition of story-telling: "An oracle and bringer of joy, the storyteller is the living memory of her time, her people. She composes on life but does not lie, for composing is not imagining, fancying, or inventing" (125).[2] Story-telling as truth-saying empowers where there is no power and validates individual experience in the absence of external validation:

> The bond between women and word. Among women themselves.... In this chain and continuum, I am but one link. The story is me, neither me nor mine. It does not really belong to me, and while I feel great responsibility for it...my story, no doubt, is me, but it is also, no doubt, older than me. (122-23)

There is a strong ambivalence about commenting on other women's lives, other women's realities. At best, when their stories are given to us, we are not quite sure how to handle them. We know that we must proceed with care. Their lives are our lives. Their stories become our own stories as well.

There always have been many myths about critically studying women's lives, and they persist to this day. They are that "things were/are not so bad," that "that was then, this is now," that "that would not happen here," and, finally, that "one or two extreme examples are not representative of reality." In the stories I have narrated here, there is an abundance of myths about how women's lives are supposed to be, what kinds of life events we are supposed to value. In many cases myths override reality, so that even after it becomes clear that the knight in shining armor will not materialize, the fantasy of storybook romance persists. We have seen just recently that women do continue to suffer because of sexism, in some very stark ways. In cultures where the institution of marriage is compulsory (nearly all cultures), women find that their interests are compromised in the negotiations carried out on their behalf by others. We know that recently in Afghanistan, women could not leave their homes unaccompanied, and thus often went without food and basic necessities.[3] We learn of women in India who are burned alive because they are not deemed economically or socially valuable. We learn of women who are subjected to ritual genital mutilation to ensure their value in the marriage market: It is believed that women who cannot experience sexual pleasure will prove more docile, and thus genital mutilation becomes a weapon to enforce compliance. We learn of others still whose genitals are sewn shut to ensure their sexual fidelity. Sexism and misogyny are acted out in the lives of women in many subtle and not so subtle ways. It makes sense to share the stories of individual women's lives, because that is where the truth lies. Each individual incident of oppression tells a truth about the lives of many others: "Each story is at once a fragment and a whole; a whole within a whole" (Minh-ha 123). Each individual life is reality.

Today, as a teacher at a metropolitan college, I have the privilege of listening to the life stories of students from every corner of the world. Their own narratives about their mothers, sisters, aunts and themselves spur much of my knowledge about the details of women's lives in other cultures. My Nigerian students tell me that in their native cultures, disobeying one's father in selecting a husband causes women to become disowned forever: "They might see you in a ditch and not help you. They will not know you, the rest of your life."[4] In a discussion about the "Myth of Rapunzel" exhibit at the Museum of Women in the Arts, the same group of students, African and West Indian especially, nodded in assent as one student narrated the ways in which head-shaving is used in her culture to punish unruly women. This appears to be a shared reality, and thus we are a solid community. As we share pieces of personal histories, I am reminded that "speech is the materialization, externalization, and internalization of the vibrations of forces" (Minh-ha 127). After speaking, we begin our contemplations.

Where are we now? Do we feel comfortable speaking to women of other cultures about our shared core issues?

We can speak from a place that is authentically ours but can be shared by all. We can initiate a kind of discourse that is already waiting for articulation. This articulation would include stories about the lives of women all over the globe. It would be a discussion of the many different (but sometimes all too similar) faces of aggression against women. This new discourse of Women's Studies would always be global in its perspective, encompassing a number of different languages and customs. We would have to learn and study continuously because we would need to always traverse oceans and realities to reach a greater understanding. We must, perhaps, become more comfortable with our discomfort, and we must begin to see our First World selves as "different."

## Notes

1. For example, see:

    *Opening the Gates: A Century of Arab Feminist Writing*, edited by Margot Badran and Miriam Cooke (Indiana University Press, 1990).

    *Women's Studies International: Nairobi and Beyond*, edited by Aruna Rao (The Feminist Press, 1991).

2. Trinh T. Minh-ha, *Woman, Native, Other: Writing Postcoloniality and Feminism.* Indiana University Press, 1989.

3. Some especially moving stories were shared by an Afghani member of RAWA at a presentation held on the Rockville campus of Montgomery College, September 2001.

4. Special thanks to students in Honors World Literature, EN202, Fall 2001 and Introduction to Women's Studies, WS101, Spring 2002, for sharing their knowledge and experiences so openly.

# Cuban Women: Betrayed by Revolution
## by Teresa Bevin

Throughout Cuba's history, women have waged a battle for emancipation and equal rights while enduring the culturally reinforced Cuban-style *machismo*, two wars of independence against Spanish colonialism (1868-78 and 1895-98), United States occupation (1899-1902), a long string of ineffective governments, and the revolution of 1959. By 1952 the island was ready for a transformation once more. Corrupt governments supported by the United States and exploitation of natural and human resources by American companies brought the Cuban spirit to the boiling point, and the revolutionary movement began. The island again became the site of decisive world changes. If Spain's power ended in Cuba with the second war against colonialism, Latin America's rebellion against the United States began in Cuba.

Sadly, that promising socialist revolution which initially brought dignity and sovereignty to Cubans soon became a Soviet-backed totalitarian regime under the leadership of Fidel Castro. The fall of the Soviet block left the island's economy in shambles, and today Cuba barely survives through limited trade with a few countries, tourism, and, ironically, some of the same corrupt tactics that brought about the revolution in the first place, including shameless catering to foreigners and prostitution. The economic blockade enforced by the United States has further isolated Cuba from much of the world and given Fidel Castro the perfect excuse behind which to hide the regime's mismanagement of resources.

With the triumph of Castro's revolution, the women's movement in Cuba took a unique direction. The "new" Cuban ideology rejected values that promoted status-seeking, individualism, and achievements other than those that contributed directly to the agenda created by the regime. The Federation of Cuban Women, born with the revolution, enjoyed support and encouragement from the leadership within the context of egalitarian values. This meant that instead of fighting the government for recognition of their demands for equality, the Federation sought freedom from capitalistic domination and the cultural trail it left behind after capitalistic endeavors were eradicated from the island. The Federation aided the regime in its successful international propaganda machine, but in reality, the only female to hold any position of apparent power within the Cuban government is Vilma Espín, the president of the Federation and the wife of Raúl Castro, Fidel's brother. Her role, in essence, is that of "first lady" and nothing more.

However, a less public battle for equality had been brewing throughout the ongoing "revolution," one fought on the home front within the parameters of a society whose goals are prescribed by a government led exclusively by males. That smaller battle, slow in gaining momentum, has been sadly undermined today in the name of basic survival.

## The Promise

Millions initially benefited from the social changes brought about by the revolution. Those who lived in remote regions many miles away from the nearest school soon began to witness the transformation. "Forts and military bunkers will become schools" was the promising slogan. During the first three decades of the revolution, illiteracy was declared a thing of the past, and everyone could pursue an education free of charge. Therefore, as I reflect in *Havana Split*, "many sharp minds that would have been wasted under previous governments, because of class and race discrimination, flourished after the triumph of the revolution" (Bevin, 1998, p. 154).

The Cuban revolution presented a well-publicized campaign for the validation and education of the poor, blacks and women. The Cuban people would be an educated people, the masters of their destinies. Slogans appeared everywhere in the streets, on television, newspapers and magazines. Cubans would be politically savvy, articulate, and able to discover for themselves the trappings of corrupt political systems. No Cuban ever would be exploited again, women never would be second-class citizens, and they never would be forced to sell their bodies to rich foreigners. The traditional "pleasers" that routinely brought American businessmen to the Cuban shores for short escapades, weekends, or overnight trysts ended swiftly. No more casinos and no more clubs staffed by the "high-class" prostitutes that had contributed to Havana's dubious fame ever would exist again on Cuban soil. The culture of servitude among the poor was over. In exchange, all physical and intellectual efforts would be directed to the benefit and support of the revolution. The work and sacrifice of able-bodied citizens would bring liberty and prosperity to all.

Idealistic Cubans, dazed by Castro's brilliant rhetoric, swallowed the hook and surrendered to the demands of the revolution. All their prayers seemed to have been answered. But in time, even prayers would become one of the bases of discontent. The so-called revolution soon ceased revolutionizing social structures and began to undermine and erode them under the guise of reforms aimed at social equality. "Revolution" may have been the right term for what was happening in Cuba up to the late sixties, but in time it has become a misnomer. The revolution turned into devolution.

## Promise Fulfilled?

Today's Cuban population is internationally recognized as one of the best educated of not just Latin America, but the world. Illiteracy is virtually non-existent, and most youngsters are encouraged to embark on a career, though the field one may pursue is not always chosen by the student, but by a panel of advisors that determine what is most necessary at any particular time, with little thought for the student's inherent aptitudes and desires. Over half of all Cubans have become skilled technicians, physicians, scientists, teachers, and specialists of all kinds regardless of gender and race.

Until the dissolution of the Soviet Union, university students were often sent to its member countries to further their studies, with all expenses paid by Cuba and/or the Soviet Union. Afterwards, students would complete supervised internships in remote villages of Africa, Central and South America and serve as eager "missionaries" of revolution in the process. It did not matter that educational material given in class was slanted toward the views of the regime, and literature available to students or to any citizen was, and still is, strictly controlled. No progressive literature from the "outside" was allowed in libraries and bookstores, all owned and sponsored by the regime. Young men and women of the poorest neighborhoods and of the most remote villages enjoyed equal rights to an education, and this reality went very far in the hearts of many Cubans, as it gained international praise for the regime. All Cuban citizens, young and old, were expected to complete the sixth grade and were strongly encouraged to finish high school. Cuban women benefited greatly from the regime's thrust toward education. Many learned about their true worth and the role they could have in society beyond that of nurturers. Scores of women joined the militia and the Communist Party, many as a way of paying for the education they were receiving. They became soldiers ready to defend the revolution that had given them dignity and self-worth.

## The Family at Risk

In time, the same revolutionary government that had elevated the dispossessed, the exploited, and for all appearances, women, to a "privileged" position as recipients of the best the revolution had to offer, began to wage a silent attack at the fabric of Cuban society. The family, both nuclear and extended, was perceived as a hindrance to the revolution because it was based on loyalty among its members. As I note in *Parenting in Cuban-American Families*, "Because the basic social unit for Cubans is the extended family, regardless of how fragmented by distance this network might be, kinship among its members may reach far and wide, granting support and a sense of belonging, even in exile" (Bevin, 2001, p. 182). Under the new dictatorship there could be no other loyalty than that expressed toward the regime. Affiliations to church, family, and social organizations were targeted as being in opposition to the rule. As a result, what took place in the name of social change was instead a steady decline of family life and principles and the militarization of schools. In contrast to the slogan of the early sixties, schools were becoming more like forts and military bunkers where youngsters spent a great deal of their daily lives.

Though rhetoric was appealing, the ideas inspired and attractive, they inevitably backfired when put into practice. Some believed Castro's promises that the temporary sacrificial period would result in a better future, while many soon became disenchanted. Family structures began to crumble under the pressure of differing ideologies. Estrangement among siblings and between the old and young became commonplace. Religious practices, which always were a major source of support for the Cuban family, soon were equated with counterrevolutionary activities. Not only did the predominant Roman Catholic church suffer, but so did *Santería*, a mixture of African mythology and Catholic rituals practiced by blacks and whites alike in which female *orishas* (priestesses) enjoyed equal prestige with their male counterparts.

A slew of ordinances was established that accentuated the sacrifice of all for the benefit of all, most resulting in further erosion of family unity. The government mandated that citizens perform "voluntary work." This meant that all adults had to work in the sugar-cane fields and coffee plantations in order to keep their current jobs and revolutionary status. Those who did not cooperate with the nation's "glorious destiny" were publicly criticized and deemed to be suspect of counterrevolutionary leanings. Many remained in jails for decades, classified as traitors because they refused to work for the government.

Because few married couples worked in the same place, long separations were inevitable. University, college, and high-school students joined their government-integrated schools in the countryside to perform agricultural labor. My high school was no exception. From age fourteen until I finally was able to leave the island at eighteen, I spent two to three months a year in labor camps with my classmates. The work varied greatly. Sometimes students were assigned the task of removing rocks from a field as preparation for plowing, or we would plant trees, pick coffee, or dig up sweet potatoes. Children and youngsters were housed in leaky military barracks, fed a diet of starches, often rancid and maggot-ridden, and forced to march in military formation to and from the fields, where work was to begin at dawn and finish at dusk. My father and older brother, both professionals, joined their co-workers in the harvest of sugarcane. My mother, a former dental technician turned housewife, was left alone months at a time, forced to attend "block meetings" and take turns to "guard" the neighborhood throughout the night. Women were required to report on other neighbors' ins and outs and to walk the streets with baseball bats in their hands. These practices were absurd and laughable, but the regime took them very seriously. Those who accused others of counterrevolutionary activities, such as hosting gatherings at home without permission or acquiring black-market goods, were rewarded with praise and recognition among the new elite. For women who had seldom been properly recognized for their efforts in managing a home and raising their families, this praise was welcome and sought out.

In the meantime, "infant circles" were created so that mothers could leave their youngest children in a safe place while they surrendered themselves to the service of the revolution. It was in these infant circles that communist indoctrination began for Cuban toddlers. Elementary school children were a population in between, and retired grandparents and other older relatives were expected to assume a parenting role while the younger parents were in labor camps. In short, institutionalized involvement of every family member in the creation of the new society relegated family unity to a secondary position. The new society was based on the revolution alone. Thus began the emotional erosion of Cuban women at all levels; grandmothers, mothers, young women, and girls saw their worlds turn upside down. No longer were they the glue that maintained the integrity of family structure. No longer could they count on watching their children grow while educating them their own way. Their children, too, were the children of the revolution, and they would grow up without spiritual beliefs, united in hatred and anger by the leader against the one aggressor: the imperialism of the United States. The slogan was, and is, "Cuban women, on guard!"

## Historical Perspective

Throughout the many upheavals suffered by this small nation, and prior to the first war of independence of 1868, Cuban women have struggled to maintain the family structure. One of many of these early examples can be found in the writings of my great-great-grandmother, Encarnación de Varona (1835-1888), who maintained a journal before, during and after the first Cuban War of Independence (González, 1990). Throughout her account the struggle of this matriarch to maintain her sense of self-worth and the integrity of her family can be appreciated. When Encarnación was four years old, she lost her mother in child-birth, though her baby brother survived. Her widowed father, always traveling on business to support the children, could not devote time to her. She stated that having no father to protect her as she grew up, nor the love of a mother, she quickly learned to rely upon herself. She lived in several extended-family households, often separated from her younger brother, feeling unloved and unwanted, an orphan living off the charity of others. But in her own words, she "developed self-love, a need to maintain her dignity in the face of temptation and men's 'selfish ways,' and the drive to increase her knowledge in a man's world" (de Varona, 1880). She later struggled between her patriotic feelings and her love for her children. With great distress she watched her sons join the march to the countryside to fight against the Spanish army, where she lost her youngest. She kept busy to forget her pain, initiating a literacy campaign on her own and teaching anyone who wanted to learn how to read, especially women. She believed that the education of women was the only hope for peace. Today, her journals are available for research in Cuban historical archives, where they are regarded as a vivid example of true womanly grit. But she was not unique among Cuban women at that, or at any other, time.

Cuban women often have been forced into salient roles of activists instrumental in all insurrection movements. Through armed confrontations, general strikes, and urban disturbances, Cuban women have formed coalitions and clandestine associations and poured into the streets to claim their rights, rally for an end to government corruption, or demand food to feed their families. Hundreds of women fought alongside Castro's men on Cuba's eastern mountains, but none made the transition into the government elite with the exception of Celia Sánchez, Castro's partner, who stayed by his side until her death but held no official rank.

## Machismo, Before and After

Before the revolution, women had been the center of the home, and as such they were in full charge of their children. Many, however, especially the poor, were undeniably exploited by society, while many in the middle to upper classes were emotionally abused by womanizing husbands. It was seen as normal for men of a certain position to have a mistress, while wives looked the other way and pretended not to know in order to save their dignity. Physical abuse was not a documented problem before the revolution, however. Within Cuba's macho society, boys learned that overpowering a weaker person was unmanly and dishonorable. They were taught to defend their sisters with courage (Bevin, 2001, p199), and to come to the aide of any woman. But according to reporter Pedro Juan Gutiérrez (1999), Cubans living on the island today seem to have abandoned these traditions. Mutual abuse in couples is becoming more commonplace. Gutiérrez states that this has been exacerbated by the lack of housing that forces couples to live in crowded conditions, and by the new role that many women have assumed in order to help their families survive a collapsed economy. Through prostitution many Cuban women are able to provide their families with basic necessity items. Very few relationships are able to survive these arrangements and violence is often the result.

## Women in Exile

The new militaristic system of surveillance and repression created a population of soldiers and dressed most working women in militia uniforms, thus minimizing their Caribbean sensuality. The new society was set in place. Couples were kept apart weeks at a time, and children did not see their parents on a regular basis. The transformation was swift and painful. Cubans began to leave the country by hundreds of thousands in search of freedom to live their own lives and found themselves facing another kind of struggle. Because, as I've noted elsewhere, "uprooting produces its own form of grief, one endured away from familiar environments and support systems and thus resistant to resolution" (Bevin, 2001, p. 181), the issue of survival in a foreign land becomes even more difficult.

The experience of exile varied according to the period in which it occurred, as there have been several distinct waves of Cuban exiles coming into the United States. Each wave presented its own unique form of hardship for Cuban women. The first waves of exiles in 1959 and 1961 were mostly composed of members of the upper middle-class. Most of these exiles left the island with only the clothes on their backs and were forced to join the labor force in the United States at its lowest levels, which was unfamiliar to them. Lucky were the families who could cross the Florida Strait together, as roughly half those who left Cuba after the revolution had to leave their families behind in order to claim spouses, children, and parents as soon as they could afford the paper work and plane fares. Fichu Menocal, a member of the former bourgeoisie who chose to remain in Cuba, stated:

> We don't mind so much having to start somewhere else, having lost this or that. What we are always sad about is the loss of togetherness, the way of Cuban families. The disruption, being apart, was really most painful. (Geldoff, 1992, p.15)

Subsequent waves of exiles were essentially middle-class citizens who had to struggle with arbitrary emigration laws set up by the Cuban government. Most of these individuals had to wait for permission to exit the country while working in labor camps. They suffered untold humiliations and were kept separated from their children and spouses until they were able to leave the island. Once in the United States, they struggled to adapt and survive. For the women it was particularly difficult. They often found employment sooner than the men, but the men were more likely to obtain clerical jobs that did not involve cleaning or care-giving.

Because of the stress imposed by the hardships of starting anew, away from familiar support systems, the childbirth rate among them dropped significantly. Low fertility rates have been found to "reflect the disruptive impact of migration" (Suárez, 1998, p. 180). This is thought to be the consequence of "a natural decrease in sexual drive caused by the stress of adapting to a new environment combined with long working hours" (Bevin, 2001, p. 188). But in the case of Cuban women, the low rate in childbirth helped them concentrate on other endeavors, such as careers and occupations. Furthermore, the fear of jeopardizing their ability to make an adequate living and prepare the way for more relatives to come from Cuba may be at the heart of further delays in procreation.

Traditionally, and without relation to post-revolution propaganda, Cubans, both males and females, are expected to be successful in their studies and at work. Their work ethics are strong, and their expectations for a good education have transcended the hardships of exile. A comfortable lifestyle is a must, and no sacrifice is too harsh in order to attain it. In Cuban-American households, women work as hard and as long as the men. Women born in Cuba are painfully aware of what they lost to the revolution and what they left behind. They lost a perfect climate and close, warm friendships and family relations. The general thrust among them was to recover all that and more. Cubans believe that those things which cannot be duplicated can be improved. The road is long and painful, but the rewards are many, and Cuban women on the whole are very proud of who they are and where they come from.

## The Betrayal

In 1959 and throughout the sixties, Cuba was hailed as an example for Latin America to follow. Today, forty-three years later, Cuba is the saddest example of human rights violations in the Americas. Not because of the poverty and squalor, which can easily be found to equal or worse degrees in other Latin American countries, but because Cuba has endured a so-called "revolution" of forty-three years that was supposed to end all that. And worst of all is what has happened to the women. The beauty of the best educated women in Latin America is now for sale to tourists with dollars in their pockets. The betrayal of Cubans by the revolution is complete.

The Cuban economy is in shambles at best, and non-existent at worst. The regime has managed, nevertheless, to attract and maintain American currency on the island with the help of Cuban-Americans who send money to their starving relatives and through the appeal of magnificent Cuban beaches to tourists from Canada, Spain, Italy, and Latin-America. But underneath it all is what amounts to the traffic of *mulatas* (brown women). Cuban women are sought out by Spaniards, Canadians, Italians, and Latin-Americans alike, but among those women, *mulatas* are preferred for their exotic beauty. Prostitution is supposedly illegal, but government officials look the other way when students between seventeen and nineteen years old and young women in their twenties line the streets most frequented by tourists in the hopes of making a catch. The typical "catch" is a middle-aged business man with extra dollars to spare. Any man fitting this description can choose among the youngest and most beautiful of women. Most of these girls and women see no other way out of squalor than selling their bodies in order to supply their homes, and often their husbands and children, with badly needed goods that are only available in exchange for dollars. These women are called *jineteras* (jockeys).

As a lure to foreign visitors, the Cuban regime sponsors a web site whose name is changed periodically due to international outrage, but its name at the time of this writing is http://www.Cubanaffairs.com. This web site is used to display photographs and measurements of young Cuban women (Candelario, 2000). There are similar web sites where Filipino, Russian, and Thai young women are on display, but Cuba has quickly become the jewel in the crown of this international system of sexual exploitation of women. Nobody could have thought that the glorious Cuban revolution that has inspired so many around the world would place their brightest and most beautiful women on the auction block, with blessings. Thousands of women have agreed to display their charms on the internet in the hopes that a wealthy foreigner will take notice and come to the island to fall in love with them and take them away where they can find a better future. Sadly, hundreds of them have encountered humiliation at best, and foul play at worst in countries where they have no name, support systems, or identity numbers. They have been taken as merchandise, used, and discarded by unscrupulous characters.

The process of "acquiring" a young Cuban woman is very simple. The "buyer" opens an account with the agency and "clicks" for information. The agency explains all possible routes of travel to Cuba, provides an estimate of expenses, and even offers a "guide" upon arrival. The photos of these women smile at the viewer from their position of desperation, and the match is completed. No comment is ever made about the women's real intentions to escape their misery. They claim to be searching for "the man of their dreams." No Cuban male could fit that description under the present circumstances. The foreigner makes a selection, travels to Cuba, and meets his "girlfriend." If he likes her, he must pay for her paperwork, leave the country, and then send for her. She enters the mouth of the shark filled with hope, but alone and scared.

*Jineteras* between fifteen and thirty years old walk the streets and give themselves to foreigners freely, in exchange for dollars, clothes, shoes, and food for their families. They have no plans for the future, as they only hope to survive today and provide for their loved ones. They prostitute themselves in the name of survival. All revolutionary ideals or thoughts of emancipation have been lost for them, and only the most primitive of instincts remains.

Cuba is on the verge of change once more amidst differing currents. The United States continues to enforce the economic embargo against Cuba in spite of international pressure to loosen the grip. This effort to isolate the island has never worked except as evidence in favor of Castro's argument that the United States is ultimately responsible for his people's misery.

Today, young Cubans feel betrayed by the inability of the regime to deliver on its promises. "What about us," they may ask themselves. "Why can't we have hope for a better future?" Family ties have been severed, the people humiliated, traditions lost. But this resilient country will rise again. The Cuban people are educated and knowledgeable. Their sacrifices have made them resourceful, inventive, and strong. In spite of family dismemberment due to affiliation and exile, the nuclear family in Cuba remains strong in the face of financial ruin for the country. When the change finally comes and the dust settles, the women will again take an active part in the re-shaping of a new society, a society where they can be the creators of their own destiny.

## References

Bevin, T. (1998). *Havana Split.* Houston, Texas: Arte Público Press.

Bevin, T. (2001). Parenting in Cuban-American families. In N. B. Webb, (Ed.). *Biulturally diverse parent-child and family relationships* (pp. 181-201). New York: Columbia University Press.

Candelario, A. (2000). *A new form of sexual exploitation in Cuba: Women "to order"* (pp. 4-11). Carta de Cuba, la escritura de la libertad. San Juan, Puerto Rico. Vol. Fall-Winter 2000.

de Varona, E. (1880). *Archivos de la ciudad de Camagüey, Cuba.* Biblioteca Nacional José Martí.

Geldoff, L. (1992). *Cubans: Voices of change.* New York: St. Martin's Press.

González, M. (1990). *La vida pública y secreta de Encarnación de Varona* Revista de la Biblioteca Nacional José Martí. Vol. 2.

Gutiérrez, P. J. (1999). *Dirty Havana Trilogy.* New York: Farrar, Straus and Giroux.

Suárez, Z. E. (1998). Cuban-American families. In R. W. Habenstein, C. H. Mindel, and R. Wright, Jr. (Eds.). *Ethnic Families in America* (pp. 172-98). Upper Saddle River, NJ: Prentice Hall.

# Women's Work: Environmental Activism in India and Kenya

by Dianne Ganz Scheper

## Introduction

"Resource depletion"—an abstract enough concept to most of us in the West— is a painfully pressing reality to many thousands of poor women in areas of the Third World where Western-style development projects are destroying local environments and creating human misery on an appalling scale. In these regions under development, the people most affected are the poorest of the poor— primarily peasants and rural peoples who depend solely on rivers, farmlands and forests for their livelihoods. Because it is the woman's role in these communities to grow the family vegetables and gather firewood and water, it is women who bear the brunt of the hardships when these vital resources dwindle and disappear.

What is remarkable—and the subject of this essay—is that a number of these women have banded together in surprisingly effective ways to fight against the destruction of the rivers and forests on which their communities depend. Despite the fact that they live in cultures which have traditionally denied them political participation, they are standing up against powerful corporate forces, even when doing so subjects them to intimidation, humiliation, and danger. And they are forging a new brand of environmental activism which has won the admiration of people the world over.

This essay documents the ongoing struggles as of this writing (in 2002) of three such activist groups and tells the stories of the women who have inspired and organized them: the Chipko Andolan (Tree-hugging Movement) in the Himalayan foothills of Northwest India; the Narmada Bachao Andolan (Save the

Narmada River Movement) in Central India; and the Green Belt Movement in Kenya. [1]

Before embarking on their stories, however, we need to understand something of the situations that have given rise to these resistance movements: the human and ecological tragedies that are being wrought in the name of "development." And we need to recognize why, from the perspective of these Third World women, development is a highly dubious enterprise—not a method of creating wealth, as many in the West believe, but a euphemism, really, for transferring resources from native peoples to private, multi-national interests, from the poor to the already wealthy.

### The Cost of Developing Natural Resources: Who Pays?

Simi Lal, an elderly peasant woman who lives in Madhya Pradesh, remembers the days when her family sat down to meals of dal, fresh vegetables, and roti. [2] That was before the building of the Bargi reservoir, part of a huge damming project under construction along the Narmada River in Central India. Now the small farms that once supplied beans and cabbages and rice for local families are underwater. The men have left the village and gone to Jabalpur, the nearest city, where they pull rickshaws, and the women are left to feed their families by selling firewood. Although they sometimes put in sixteen-hour days, the money they earn provides only the barest amount of the cheapest rice ("They Only 'Hold Pen'" 3).

Simi Lal is one of approximately thirty million Indian people who have been displaced by hydroelectric damming projects in the last fifty years (Roy, *Cost of Living* 17). Most of the displaced are peasant and tribal people, who are driven into abject poverty as a result, pulling rickshaws in nearby cities or providing cheap labor in factories. The human cost of these dams has been terrific, and so has the ecological damage, as the recent report of the World Commission on Dams makes clear. [3] The report provides detailed evidence that dams are responsible for the destruction of forests, farmlands, and wetlands, the extinction of fish and birds in the floodplains, the erosion of coastal deltas, and the emission of greenhouse gases. The Commission concludes that "the benefits of these dams have largely gone to the already well-off, while poorer sectors of society have borne the costs" (Pottinger 1).

Hydroelectric dams are just one of many Third World development projects that have impoverished both the land and rural peoples. Other projects undertaken in the name of Western-style corporate development have done likewise. Farmlands that have been held in common for centuries have been privatized to grow cash crops for profit, forcing peasants who once were farmers to work on sugarcane plantations for low wages and to depend on the company store to buy the foodstuffs that they once grew themselves. On these plantations, the stress of mono-cropping eventually degrades the soil and the chemical fertilizers poison the rivers. When nearby streams dry up or go saline, it is the poor, who cannot afford to sink wells and who depend on streams for their drinking water, whose water supplies are threatened. The shortage of water is particularly hard on women and young girls, who are the traditional water-gatherers for their families and who must walk many extra miles each day in search of groundwater that is fit for drinking. In India, low-caste women, who have no wells of their own, must frequently carry their water vessels to the wells of upper-caste women and wait patiently for some charitable upper-caste woman to fill them (Agarwal 13).

Perhaps nothing has been more destructive to the lives of the rural poor than deforestation, for forests are their communities' life-support systems. Forests supply wood for their cooking fires, fodder for the family livestock, fruits for their tables, and herbs for their medicines. Since gathering firewood and fodder is traditionally "women's work" in these communities, when nearby forests are felled for timber export, it is the women who bear the heaviest burden, for they must travel long distances in search of wood. In Northwest India and East Africa, there are women who now spend over half of their time foraging, sometimes walking as far as 12 kilometers a day. Often their search is fruitless, yielding little more than shrubs and tree roots, which do not provide adequate fuel. As one Indian woman puts it, it is no longer "what's in the pot that worries you, but what's under it" (Agarwal 14).

Another Indian woman from Uttar Pradesh in Northern India remembers poignantly when it was otherwise:

> When we were young, we used to go to the forest early in the morning without eating anything. There we would eat plenty of berries and wild fruits [and] drink the cold sweet [water] of the Banji [oak] roots... In a short while we would gather all the fodder and firewood we needed, rest under the shade of some huge tree and then go home. Now, with the going of the trees, everything else has gone too (quoted in Agarwal 13).

In these countries, the shortage of firewood can also be a cause of family malnutrition and sickness. To conserve firewood, women must frequently feed their families less nutritious foods that don't require cooking or serve partially cooked foods or leftovers, both of which are risky alternatives in a tropical climate where food can easily spoil. Though there are not yet any conclusive studies about the impact of fuel shortage in India or East Africa, studies in rural Bangladesh show the number of meals eaten daily and the number of cooked meals both declining (Agarwal 14).

It is not simply nutrition that is declining in these communities; it is the whole structure of family life. Men leave the village to look for work in the cities, and their absence means an increased workload for the women who remain to care for their families. The women who spend inordinate hours foraging for wood often must leave their younger children unattended at home. Tensions erupt between wives and their mothers-in-law, who remember how abundant the forests were in their youth, and who lay the blame for the scarcity on the ineptitude of their daughters-in-law. These accumulated pressures have led to an increase in substance abuse and domestic violence, as well as an increasing incidence of suicide (Rawat 2).

Like the proverbial canaries in the coal mines, these women are showing us the early and devastating human effects of environmental degradation. But, as we noted in the introduction, they are showing us something else, besides. They are demonstrating how, even against heavy odds, women can join together to defend the integrity of their homelands and the dignity of their way of life.

We turn now to the accounts of three such resistance efforts: the Chipko Movement, the Save the Narmada Movement, and the Green Belt Movement. Each of these movements has developed its own distinctive strategies and signature methods; however, they have several things in common worth noting at the onset. First, while these are primarily women's movements, they don't exclude males; indeed, in the case of the Chipko movement, men have provided leadership roles. Second, all three movements are conscientiously non-violent. The Indian movements are modeled on Gandhi's principle of *satyagraha*, or non-violent protest, and the Greenbelt movement in Kenya, while not explicitly Gandhian, is equally committed to nonviolence, in spite of the fact that its leaders have been physically beaten and jailed. Third, and crucially important, one of the significant by-products of the movements is the schooling of women in the ABC's of organized political participation. In cultures where women traditionally have no political power, these women are discovering the value of women's solidarity. As Wangari Maathai, the founder of the Kenyan Green Belt movement has observed, "When you organize people to plant trees you are also planting ideas for organizing."

Finally, all three movements and their leaders have won international recognition. All three are recipients of the prestigious Right Livelihood Award (sometimes referred to as the alternative Nobel Prize), which honors organizations and individuals who offer "practical and exemplary answers to the crucial problems facing the world today" and who "show that problems which often look intractable can be confronted by individuals or small groups acting together and mobilizing others for the common good."[4]

## Chipko Andolan and the Himalayan Forests

The oldest of the women's environmental movements is the Chipko Andolan, the "tree-hugging movement." Its legendary founder, Amrita Devi, was an ordinary woman who is said to have defied a Maharajah in Rajasthan over three hundred years ago. The Maharajah had given an order to cut down the sacred *khejri* trees in a forest near his palace. But when the axemen arrived at the forest, so the story goes, Amrita Devi gathered the women of her village and instructed them to protect the trees by "embracing them" (in Hindi, *chipko*). The wood cutters left the scene, and in that moment, the inspiration for the Chipko movement was born (Shiva, *Staying Alive* 67).[5]

Now, three centuries later, the Chipko movement has become an icon of Third World feminist environmental activism. Although its two most public leaders, C.P. Bhatt and Sundarial Bahuguna, are male, it is women who provide the real backbone of the movement and who figure most prominently in its richly-storied history. Two of these women, Mira Behn and Sarala Behn, both close disciples of Gandhi, between them forged the two-fold focus that has become the Chipko trademark: a respect for local ecology and a recognition of the power that women can wield when they organize on behalf of social issues.

The ecological focus is a legacy of Mira Behn, who lived in an ashram in the 1940's, close to where the Ganges flows down from the Himalayan mountains. She had moved there to study cattle raising (in Gandhi's words, to "serve the cow"), since cows are essential to small, subsistence farming. But Behn turned her attention from tending cattle to ecology when she experienced the devastating floods that inundated the region each summer, sweeping away trees, villagers' homes, and even their cattle. She soon discovered the cause of the flooding. The hills upstream were practically denuded. The thick, broad-leaf forests had been cut down and replanted with shallow-rooted pine trees which were being harvested by contractors for their resin. Behn went to local peoples to learn what species of trees were native to the region and how people had used the forests. She determined that the primary reason for the erosion was the disappearance of the local *banj* (or oak) trees, and that the solution was not merely planting any kind of tree, but planting "ecologically appropriate trees." Mira Behn argued for environmental programs combining agriculture, forestry and animal husbandry, and though her programs were not immediately established, her ecological insights have lived on in Chipko philosophy (Shiva, *Staying Alive* 69-71; Lane 3 ).

It was Sarala Behn, who had worked with Gandhi in the Independence Movement, who gave women of the region their first experience of the political power of non-violent protests. In the 1960's, she mobilized them to protest the abusive use of alcohol among the men of their villages who "earned cash incomes from felling trees with one hand and lost the cash to liquor with the other." Under Sarala Behn's leadership, thousands of women picketed the government shops that sold alcohol, successfully challenging both the government and their husbands (Shiva, *Staying Alive* 72; Lane 4).

Inspired by their success in these prohibition campaigns, the women of the Himalayas were ready a decade later, in the 1970's, to challenge the corporate interests that continued to threaten their forests. Over the years, natural disasters in the Himalayas had multiplied, as commercial contractors stepped up their assaults on the hills, clear-cutting the forests and blasting mountainsides for limestone. According to one report, "the hum of machinery, rumble of construction vehicles, and explosion of dynamite [had become] ubiquitous" (Rawat 3-4). By the early seventies, it seemed clear to the hill people that something had to be done to stop the relentless plundering of the forests.

Therefore, in March 1973, when the manufacturer of a sporting goods company attempted to cut down hundreds of ash trees for use in making tennis rackets, villagers in Uttar Pradesh staged a protest. Singing traditional songs and beating drums, they marched into the forest to "embrace the trees." Faced with this local opposition, the Simon Company left, only to reappear three months later in a village eighty-some kilometers away, where they had obtained another logging permit. But there a seventy-two year old woman, Shyama Devi, who had picketed a wine shop as part of the earlier prohibition campaign, put her activist experience to work and organized the local women. For the next six months, they "kept a vigil" in the forest to protect the trees, until the contractor finally withdrew (Shiva, *Staying Alive* 73-74; Jain, "Standing Up for Trees").

A year later, another confrontation occurred when the state announced its plan to auction off 2,500 trees in the Reni forest, overlooking the Alakananda River, one of the rivers that had erupted in raging floods only four years earlier, inundating hundreds of homes and livestock. It must have seemed obvious to everyone but the contractor that cutting down the forests above this river was an invitation to further flooding. In any case, the connection was not lost on the local peoples of the valley, who had been educated by Chipko leaders about the crucial importance of forests in preventing soil erosion.

On the day the lumber company showed up, the men of the village were away, but the Chipko women were ready to face down the lumbermen alone. Gaura Devi, a widow in her fifties, emerged as the leader on this occasion. Later, she reported: "Our men were out of the village so we had to come forward and protect the trees. We have no quarrel with anybody but we only wanted to make the people understand that our existence is tied with the forests" (Guha 159). This same Gaura Devi is reputed to have faced down a lumberman carrying a rifle with the admonition: "Brother, this forest is our *maika* (mother's home). Do not axe it. Landslides will ruin our homes and fields" (Philipose 69).[6] Under Gaura Devi's leadership, the women formed vigilance groups and took turns over the next months standing guard in the forest. As a result, the state was finally forced to set up a review committee, which ultimately issued a ten-year ban on commercial logging in the Alakananda valley.

The confrontation in the Reni forest is typical of the Chipko style of resistance. For the most part, their protests are decentralized and spontaneous. They combine peaceful demonstrations with traditional symbolic gestures, sometimes conducting fasts in the forest, sometimes tying sacred threads around the trees, as an ancient Hindu token of guardianship. Their confrontations have produced memorable bits of dialogue that add to and ornament the growing body of Chipko legends. One such encounter, in the Adwani forest in 1977, gave birth to what has since become a renowned Chipko slogan. A vexed official chastised the women for being completely ignorant of the commercial value of the forests, saying: "You foolish women. Do you know what the forests bear? Resin, timber, foreign exchange." To which the Chipko women chanted a reply:

> Yes, we know what forests bear.
> Soil, water, and pure air.
> Soil, water and pure air
> Sustain the earth and all she bears. (Shiva, *Staying Alive* 77).

Their response has since become a rallying cry for environmental movements across the globe. It is quoted wherever the Chipko movement is invoked and whenever it seems necessary to remind people that the natural world is not primarily a profit-bearing commodity, but a life-giving source that provides us with those basic essentials without which we cannot survive: soil, water, and pure air.

## Medha Patkar and the Narmada Bachao Andolan

Further south, in Central India, another fierce environmental struggle is being waged. Now in its seventeenth year, the struggle is to save the Narmada River from the largest dam development project in Indian history. The project involves building a staggering number of dams on the river: two huge "mega" dams, thirty large dams, one hundred thirty-five medium-sized dams, and as many as three thousand additional small dams. Funded by the World Bank to the tune of $450 million, the project will displace at least 300,000 people (the estimate goes as high as half a million), mostly poor peasants and *adivasis* (tribal peoples), whose families have lived along the Narmada for thousands of years.[7]

The Narmada is India's longest westward-flowing river, winding eight hundred miles from Madhya Pradesh in the east and emptying into the Arabian Sea in the west. In addition to providing water for thousands along its banks, the Narmada has enormous cultural value. It is considered one of India's holiest rivers. According to legend, Lord Shiva himself is said to have given the river its name—Narmada, the "ever-delightful." For hundreds of years, people have sought to be "blessed by the river" by making a pilgrimage along its length, a journey whose landmarks are visible today in the many temples and shrines that dot its banks. Anyone who has read Kipling's *Jungle Book* has visited the Narmada in her imagination, for the landscape of Kipling's stories is drawn from its forested hills and plains.

In 1985, Medha Patkar, a young social worker from Bombay, visited the Narmada Valley to study the impact of the largest of the dams, called Sardar Sarovar, on tribal villages that were about to be submerged. What she found appalled her. She discovered that the state was uprooting thousands more families than it had publicly acknowledged and had no plans to resettle them. She also learned that the environmental impact of the dam had not been honestly evaluated or owned up to: the loss of 33,000 acres of forests and huge chunks of prime agricultural land, the destruction of traditional fishing grounds downstream, the lowering of groundtable levels, and the increased salinity of water in the surrounding valley (Govindu 2-3).

Most alarming was the fact that the peoples whose homes were about to be submerged had no real knowledge of the fate that awaited them. Patkar was so disturbed by what she saw that she decided to give up her social work and throw in her lot with the tribal peoples. She moved in with them, learned their languages, and then began walking from village to village, wearing sneakers and a faded sari, warning people about the reality of their situation. According to Catherine Caufield, a research scholar who studies the World Bank, when Patkar committed herself to protecting the rights of the rural peoples, "the future of Sardar Sarovar was rewritten" (Caufield 11-13).

Since that time, Medha Patkar has become a symbol of hope to the threatened people of the region and a persistent thorn in the side of the World Bank and its local promoters. She has organized peaceful rallies and demonstrations. She has moved into villages slated for submergence and refused to leave, even when the waters were rising around her. Following the example of Mahatma Gandhi, she has gone on prolonged hunger strikes, fasting sometimes for three weeks at a time. She has been arrested countless times.

In 1989, the Narmada Bachao Andolan ( Save the Narmada Movement) was formed, for which Patkar is the chief strategist and spokesperson. On Christmas Day in 1990, it staged its most significant demonstration against the Sardar Sarovar, the flagship dam, in what has become known as the "Long March." Six thousand men and women set out to walk more than a hundred kilometers down the valley to the dam.[8] To show their commitment to nonviolence, the demonstrators had tied their own hands together. Halfway to the site, however, they were stopped by a police blockade. Some were beaten and arrested; others were loaded onto trucks, driven to remote places and left there. In response to this violence, Patkar and seven others embarked on a hunger strike, which lasted three weeks, drawing the attention of the international media, and turning Patkar into a national heroine. Unfortunately, the publicity didn't manage to stop the dam, although it did result in the World Bank's agreeing to an independent review of the Sardar Sarovar, one of many reviews, reassessments, and repositions that have ensued over the past decade (Roy, *Cost of Living* 38-39; Caufield 14-15).

To this date, the struggle against the Narmada Dam Project continues. Many thousands have joined the struggle, including several renowned national figures. In 1990, a revered 76 year-old spiritual leader known as Baba Amte joined the movement, and he has been by Patkar's side ever since. In a dramatic gesture, he moved his ashram to the banks of the Narmada in the path of the dam's floodwaters, and made a vow to stay there and drown, if necessary. Baba, who had already earned his country's admiration through his lifelong work with leprosy patients, said that he had decided "to devote his last years to saving the holy river" (Caufield 15).

Arundhati Roy, the Booker prize-winning author of *The God of Small Things*, has also joined the cause. She has published scathing indictments of the government's policies, calling the dam project "something akin to an undeclared civil war" being waged against Indian peoples "in the name of 'development'" (*Power Politics* 4). And she has correctly identified the vital issue at stake in this battle.

> In India over the last ten years the fight against
> the Sardar Sarovar dam has come to represent
> far more than the fight for one river. . . .
> From being a fight over the fate of a river valley it began
> to raise doubts about an entire political system.
> What is at issue now is the very nature of our democracy.
> Who owns this land? Who owns its rivers? Its forests? Its fish?
> (*Cost of Living* 9).

The question of ownership is, indeed, the live nerve at the heart of the Narmada struggle—as is true with most environmental disputes. Who owns the earth's resources: the people who depend on them or private interests? The answer to this question, it's safe to predict, will eventually determine the future of the planet. In the meantime, however, the issue of ownership continues to fuel the Narmada conflict, and while opposition to the dam is growing, the future of the river is still uncertain. Shut-downs and start-ups occur in rapid and confusing sequence and often behind a fog of political doublespeak. Nevertheless, Patkar and the people of the Narmada Andolan persevere, driven by their conviction that a victory over the dams will be a victory for a sane and sustainable economic future, one that does not exploit the earth and is fair to all peoeple.

## Wangari Maathai and Kenya's Green Belt Movement

On World Environment Day, June 5th, 1977, a small group of women from Kenya's National Council of Women planted seven trees in downtown Nairobi, calling the action "Save the Land Harambee." ("Harambee" in Swahili means "let's all pull together.") That symbolic event signaled the birth of the Green Belt Movement, which since 1977 has planted 20 million trees and established more than 3,000 tree nurseries throughout Kenya ("Kenya's Greenbelt Movement").

Its founder, Wangari Maathai [9], is a remarkable woman. She is the first East African woman to have earned a doctorate from the University of Nairobi, where she went on, in the mid-seventies, to become the University's first woman professor and (in the Department of Veterinary Anatomy) their first female department chair. In the mid-seventies, she ran for Parliament and in 1997 she stood in the national election for president. (Both candidacies failed, which is not surprising in a country where public life is dominated by men and a single party has been in power for years.) Throughout her career as an environmentalist and a political activist, Maathai has worked to promote social transformation and a truly representative democracy responsive to the needs of ordinary people. She has received numerous national and international honors, most recently the 2001 "Kenyan Community Abroad Award of Excellence" which cites her "challenges in a society where women are disadvantaged" and her "inspiration to millions of Kenyan youth, especially girls" ("Prof. Wangari Maathai: Winner").

Maathai's inspiration for the Green Belt Movement came in part from her work as a field biologist back in the seventies when she was investigating the reasons for the declining animal resistance to parasites. Wild animals were more at risk for disease, she concluded, because their habitats were being destroyed. More emphatically, Kenya was losing its forest cover.

Kenya today retains less than 2% forest cover, an alarming figure in view of the fact that, according to conservation experts, at least 10% of a country's land should be in forest cover in order to ensure an adequate water supply and prevent desertification. (Kenya's neighbor, Tanzania, in contrast, has 36% of its land in forest cover.) Because trees provide catchment areas for rain—absorbing moisture and then releasing it slowly in cycles that stimulate more rain—the shortage of trees dries out a climate, a particularly dire possibility for Kenya located as it is so close to the Sahara desert. Without trees, the rains that do come during monsoons produce flash floods and soil erosion, thereby creating a destructive cycle of flood and drought.

Recognizing the importance of trees in restoring Kenya's environment, Maathai launched the Green Belt Movement in 1977 with the initial intention of planting a million trees. She enlisted the help of small farmers to plant indigenous trees and shrubs that were appropriate for Kenya's different ecological areas. The movement grew faster than she had anticipated. By the early 1980's, they had planted nearly ten times the number she had originally intended, and had established 2,000 public green belts and some 600 tree nurseries, projects which involved several thousand women and over half-a-million school children ("Right Livelihood Award:Wangari Maathai"). To date, the Green Belt Movement has planted over twenty million trees, with the help of no fewer than 6,000 women's groups ("The Good, the Bad" 1).

Providing meaningful work for local peoples is part of the Green Belt mission. Currently, the movement employs some 80,000 people, most of them rural women. Maathai refers to the women who tend the nurseries as "foresters without diplomas." These amateur foresters encourage Kenyan farmers (70% of whom are women) to plant native species such as acacia, cedars, citrus trees, and figs (Anbarasan 6). In the late eighties, the Kenyan movement launched an All-African Network to spread environmental awareness and reforesting techniques to other African countries, such as Uganda, Ethiopia, and Zimbabwe.

The impressive achievements of the Green Belt Movement have not been without cost. Wangari Maathai and her troop of tree-planting women have been subjected to harassment and persecution by powerful factions in Kenya who oppose their efforts to protect what remains of Kenya's existing forests. In 1989, for example, the movement intervened to save Uhuru Park in Nairobi from being cut down to build a 62-story office tower, a lucrative project promoted by President Moi, Kenya's repressive and strong-armed leader. Due to the Green Belt intervention, the park was saved and has since been named a "national heritage." However, Maathai's courage in standing up to Moi's "iron regime" earned her political enemies. She has since been tear-gassed, beaten, hospitalized, and jailed. Police have broken into her home, and she regularly receives death threats. Still, undaunted, she continues her work (Mutiso 1).

In 1997, Maathai's band of tree-planters confronted riot police in order to plant trees in the Karura Forest, on the outskirts of Nairobi, where more than a third of its 2,500 acres had been sold to developers. Two years later, in January, 1999, she and a troop of thirty women, many of them grandmothers, walked into a forest outside Nairobi carrying seedlings and small hand shovels. They were planting trees to protest the scheduled destruction of the forest to create a golf course. Once again, they were confronted by Moi's hired police and beaten. But this time, Maathai had an advantage, for, unknown to the government, the event had been filmed. It drew the attention of international media and provoked a world-wide reaction strong enough to force the government to cancel the project ("The Good, the Ugly" 2).

Nevertheless, the fragile forest system in Kenya continues to be threatened. As of this writing, the government plans to excise 170,000 acres from fourteen different forests, fully one-tenth of the country's remaining 2% forest cover. Experts have predicted that such destruction would cause serious floods alternating with droughts: this, in a country that in the year 2000 experienced one of the worst droughts in its history, severe enough to cause power outages all across the country almost every day for a whole year, often throwing the country into darkness for hours on end ("Fight for the Forest" 1). In spite of such clear evidence of the dangers of deforestation, the Kenyan government seems intent on cutting down trees faster than the Green Belt Movement can possibly replenish them.

In spite of the harassment she has been subjected to, Maathai vows to continue fighting her government's wanton destruction of Kenya's forests. She continues to plant trees, which she has been doing for a quarter of a century, and she continues to struggle for greater political representation for women and other Kenyans whose interests are currently being ignored. Maathai sees the two actions, the homely act of planting trees and the struggle for political justice, as being closely interconnected. She explains the connection this way:

> The act of planting trees conveys a simple message. It suggests that at the very least you can plant a tree and improve your habitat. It increases people's awareness that they can take control of their environment, which is the first step toward greater participation in society. Since the trees we have planted are visible, they are the greatest ambassadors for our movement. (Anbarasan 2)

## Lessons from Third World Women

We in the West have much to learn from these Third World women who are struggling to protect their natural environments from exploitation. As Vandana Shiva points out, these women are not speaking merely as victims of environmental abuse, but as "voices of liberation and transformation which provide new categories of thought and new exploratory directions" (Shiva, *Staying Alive* 47). What, then, do these voices have to teach us?

Most importantly, they encourage us to think anew the whole concept of economic and environmental "development." For many Westerners, development is still an incontestable good, the doorway to universal happiness, the answer to the world's problems. These women are suggesting the opposite: that development is not the solution to the problem, but the problem, itself. Economic development for their communities has meant turning rivers into hydroelectric assembly lines, forests into timber for export, and communal farms into corporate-owned, cash-crop plantations. They see that "resource development" is usually a euphemism for "resource transfer," from the Third World to the developed world, from the poor to the already well-off, which leads very quickly to "resource depletion." (Shiva, "Development" 86).

Vandana Shiva, the physicist and eco-philosopher whose work I have cited throughout this essay, argues further that the concept of development is based on "categories of productivity and growth" which, while promoted as universal, are really parochial, belonging strictly to the Western world, and even more narrowly, to the industrial, capitalist paradigm of the last few centuries. According to this capitalist paradigm, Shiva observes, natural processes are deemed productive "only when mediated by technologies for commodity production, even when such technologies destroy life." Thus:

> A stable and clean river is not a productive resource in this view; it needs to be "developed" with dams in order to become so. . . . Natural forests remain unproductive until they are developed into monoculture plantations of commercial species. Development is thus equivalent to maldevelopment. . . . ("Development" 82)

"Maldevelopment" is precisely what these rural women-activists are resisting, the model of development that privileges the accumulation of wealth over the health of nature and human relationships. What they envision, in place of maldevelopment, is an economically and ecologically sustainable future. When Medha Patkar tells people that a victory over the dams will be a victory for sustainability, she is urging them to replace a narrow vision of development with a broader conception "based on harmonious, non-exploitative relationships between human beings and between people and nature" ("Right Livelihood Award:1991).

The contrast between maldevelopment and the women's vision of sustainability has perhaps never been put more succinctly than it was back in 1977, in that Chipko confrontation with the lumberman in the Adwani Forest. It bears repeating, for here, in a dialectical nutshell, is the ecological wisdom of these Third World women activists:

> *Lumberman:*
> You foolish women. Do you know
> what the forests bear?
> Resin, timber, foreign exchange.
>
> *Chipko women:*
> Yes, we know what forests bear.
> Soil, water, and pure air.
> Soil, water and pure air
> Sustain the earth and all she bears.

## Notes

1. Special thanks to two of my students, Lisa Shannon and Padma Soundararajan, for their contributions to this article.

2. Madhya Pradesh is a state in Central India. "Dal" is an Indian dish made of beans and "roti" is a type of bread.

3. The World Commission on Dams is an independent review body set up in 1998 to study the effectiveness of dams worldwide. Its members represent a wide spectrum of backgrounds, including the private sector, national governments, international organizations such as the World Bank, and NGO environmentalist groups. For more information on the Commission, consult <http://www.dams.org/commission/intro.htm>.

4. See "The Right Livelihood Award." <http://www.rightlivelihood.se/about.html>. It is interesting to note, incidentally, that since 1980 nearly one-third of these awards have gone to women and women's groups, in marked contrast to the Nobel Prize which is still dominated by male winners.

5. The origins of the Chipko movement are so cloaked in legend that it is difficult to establish them definitively. The account offered here is one of the most popular.

6. There are several variations in the retelling of Gaura Devi's address to the lumberman. Vandana Shiva reports Devi as saying: "This forest is our mother. When there is a crisis of food, we come here to collect grass and dry fruits to feed our children. We dig out herbs and collect mushrooms from this forest. You cannot touch these trees" (Shiva, *Staying Alive* 74).

7. The estimate of 300,000 displaced people is conservative. Some sources place the figure closer to half a million. (See Arundhati Roy, *The Cost of Living*, 34). In a 1999 interview, Medha Patkar ventured that the total number might reach 10 lakhs (1 million) people. (See Venu Govindu, "An Interview with Medha Patkar.")

8. The number of demonstrators is reported variously. Arundhati Roy in *The Cost of Living* (38-39) reports the number as 6,000. Catherine Caufield in *Masters of Illusion* (14-15) reports 3,000.

9   In 2004, after this article was written, Wangari Maathai was awarded the Nobel Peace Prize. She is the first African woman to be so honored.

## Works Cited*

Agarwal, Bina. "The Gender and Environment Debate: Lessons from India." *Feminist Studies* 18:1 (1992): 40 pp. *Academic Search Elite*: 1-32. Montgomery College, Rockville Campus Library. April 8, 2002.

Anbarasan, Ethirajan. "Wangari Muta Maathai: Kenya's Green Militant." *Unesco Courier* Dec. 1999. *InfoTrac Expanded Academic ASAP*:1-7. Gale Group. Montgomery College, Rockville Campus Library. April 8, 2002 <www.galegroup.com>.

Caufield, Catherine. *Masters of Illusion: The World Bank and the Poverty of Nations.* New York: Macmillan, 1998.

"The Fight for the Forest is Every Citizen's Duty." *Africa News Service* Nov. 2, 2001. *InfoTrac Expanded Academic ASAP*: 1-3. Gale Group. Montgomery College, Rockville Campus Library. Dec. 7, 2001 <www.galegroup.com>.

"The Good, the Bad, and the Ugly." *The Ecologist* April 2001. *InfoTrac Expanded Academic ASAP*: 1-4. Gale Group. Montgomery College, Rockville Campus Library. April 8, 2002 <www.galegroup.com>.

Govindu, Venu. "An Interview with Medha Patkar." Accessed April 28, 2002 <http://indiatogether.org/interviews/iview-mpatkar.htm>.

Guha, Ramachandra. *The UnquietWoods.* Berkeley: Univ. of California Press, 1989.

Jain, Shobita. "Standing Up for Trees: Women's Role in the Chipko Movement." *Unasylva,* No. 146: Women in Forestry. Accessed Oct. 29, 2000 <http://www.fao.org/docrep/rO465E/ro465e03.htm>.

"Kenya's Green Belt Movement." *Unesco Courier* March 1992. *InfoTrac Expanded Academic ASAP*: 1-3. Gale Group. Montgomery College, Rockville Campus Library. April 8, 2002 <www.galegroup.com>.

Lane, Carrie. "Women as the Backbone of Chipko." Accessed Oct. 29, 2000.<http://electronicsoapbox.com/es/hydepark/chipko.html>.

Mutiso, Clive. "Her Women's Army Defies an Iron Regime." *Time* Dec 14, 1998. *InfoTrac Expanded Academic ASAP*:1-2. Gale Group. Montgomery College, Rockville Campus Library. April 8, 2002<www.galegroup.com>.

Philipose, Pamela. "Women Act: Women and Environmental Protection in India." *Healing the Wounds: The Promise of Ecofeminism*. Ed. Judith Plant. Philadelphia: New Society Publishers, 1989. 67-75.

Pottinger, Lori. "Damning the Dams." *Multinational Monitor* Jan. 2001. *InfoTrac Expanded Academic ASAP*: 1-6. Gale Group. Montgomery College, Rockville Campus Library. Dec. 7, 2001 <www.galegroup.com>.

"Prof. Wangari Maathai: Winner of 2001 KCA Award of Excellence." *Africa News Service* Feb.25,2002. *InfoTrac Expanded Academic ASAP*: 1-2. Gale Group. Montgomery College, Rockville Campus Library. April 8,2002 <www.galegroup.com>.

Rawat, Rajiv. "Women of Uttarakhand: On the Frontiers of Environmental Struggle." May 1996. Accessed June 7, 2002 <http://www.bostonglobalaction.net/UK//chipko.html>.

"The Right Livelihood Award." Accessed June 7, 2002 <http://www.rightlivelihood.se/about.html>.

"The Right Livelihood Award: Wangari Maathai/Green Belt Movement (1984)." Accessed June 7, 2002 <http://www.rightlivelihood.se/recip1984 4.html>.

Roy, Arundhati. *The Cost of Living*. New York: Modern Library, 1999.

———. *Power Politics*, 2nd ed. Cambridge, Mass: South End Press, 2001.

Shiva, Vandana. *Staying Alive; Women, Ecology and Development*. London: Zed Books, 1989.

———. "Development, Ecology, and Women." *Healing the Wounds: The Promise of Ecofeminism*. Ed. Judith Plant. Philadelphia: New Society Publishers, 1989. 80-90.

"They Only 'Hold Pen'" *The New Internationalist*, July 2001. *InfoTrac Expanded Academic ASAP*: 1-6. Gale Group. Montgomery College, Rockville Campus Library. Dec. 7, 2001 <www.galegroup.com>.

\* Inclusive on-line page numbers for articles from databases are given immediately following the title of the database.

# Where Are the Women in Women's Health?
## by Maureen Edwards

Why women's health? The feminist in me is tempted to answer, "Well, why not women's health?" In fact, there are sound and salient reasons to support a study of women's health issues. First and foremost, men and women are different. I'll bet most of us have even noticed this by about age two. For example, women are about twice as likely to suffer from depression, three times more likely to have irritable bowel syndrome and about fifteen times more likely to suffer from thyroid disease than their male counterparts. Heart disease is the major killer of both men and women in this country, yet women are twice as likely to die following that first heart attack. Why is this so? Because physicians are not trained to recognize the "atypical" heart disease symptoms in women. A 1995 Gallup Poll indicated that one out of three primary care physicians were unaware of the fact that heart disease is the number one killer of women as well as men. Consequently, women are treated less aggressively than men and run a greater risk of dying. Women also have been excluded from major research initiatives. For example, The Multiple Risk Factor Intervention Trial (MR. Fit), which looked at the link between heart disease, cholesterol level and behavior, included 15,000 men but no women. One of the most respected studies of the aging process, The Baltimore Longitudinal Study of Aging begun in 1958, did not include women until 1978. Ironic, considering women live on the average seven years longer than men.

For the sake of brevity, I will refrain from mentioning all the studies that exclude women. Instead, I will take the easy approach and discuss the major studies that focus solely on the health of women. Relax: there are only two shining examples. The Nurses' Health Study begun in 1976 used a mail survey to examine the relationship between life style and health problems. Why were nurses recruited for this groundbreaking study? The most obvious answer is that nurses are an integral part of the medical profession and understand the value of research. One can conclude, therefore, that nurses are more likely to respond to the questionnaire and remain part of the study over time. A more cynical answer would be that nurses are convenient; a medical researcher would not need to go very far to recruit nurses. Still, the question remains: can the behaviors and health problems of nurses be generalized to the rest of the female population? Does advanced education and training in health and medicine give nurses an advantage not shared by the rest of us? Since they see the end result of negative health behaviors like smoking and lack of exercise on the hospital wards and in the doctors' offices every day, might they not be more inclined to change their own behaviors?

The second major study in the area of women's health is the Women's Health Initiative. The birth of this study took place in the political arena rather than the laboratory. In 1989, the General Accounting Office (GAO) of the United States Government issued a report which pointed an accusatory finger at the National Institutes of Health for failing to implement its own policy of including women in research studies. In the later part of 1990, the Congressional Caucus for Women's Issues requested a GAO investigation of how NIH was implementing their policy of female inclusion. Although the policy was in place, it appeared that it was being largely ignored. Based on this information, three months later the Women's Health Equity Act was passed and NIH established the Office of Research on Women's Health. It was from this office that the Women's Health Initiative was launched in 1991. This study focused on the health of postmenopausal women. The objective was to improve the health of this group of women through the prevention of chronic disease. So the history of research in women's health stands on a foundation of basically two pillars, one including younger women and one including older women. Is this not a sad state of affairs?

Another reason to study women's health involves the length of the female life span. Since women live an average of six to seven years longer than men, it makes economic sense to help keep women healthy. The longer an individual lives, the more likely it is she will develop a chronic disease. Chronic diseases like arthritis or osteoporosis are by definition incurable and often involve frequent intervention by the health care system. This intervention is costly both in terms of dollars and human suffering. By increasing the number of healthy, productive years a woman enjoys, society is helping to reduce the stress on an already overburdened health care system. The final consideration to be addressed here is one of equity. If women are afforded equal protection under the law, should we not also be assured of equal representation in health care research? Since women evidence differing patterns of morbidity and mortality, isn't it in society's best interest to investigate what is making women ill and what is ultimately killing us?

Following this line of reasoning, the question remains: why were women excluded from the research in the first place? Although some may suggest that much of the early work was done by male researchers who purposely excluded women, I prefer to take a more benign view. I think it was and perhaps still is a combination of convenience and concern. The simple biological fact that women have monthly hormonal cycles makes us physiologically more complex in many ways. It is more difficult to track the effects of a drug or a medical treatment in light of rising and falling hormone levels. Effects and side effects may not be as clear-cut in female subjects as in male. OK, the job is more difficult, but this does not mean that it cannot be done. I think we need to acknowledge the difficulties and continue on with our work. And yes, women do have babies, another fact not lost on the average person. But fear of harming the woman or the unborn child is not sufficient reason to exclude women from research protocols. To do so not only infantilizes women and insults our common sense, but, more importantly, it places our health and well being at risk. Pregnancy can be avoided during the course of a study if women are informed of why it is important to do so and how it may be done. In a worst-case scenario in which a pregnant woman is exposed to an experimental drug or treatment, is it not of vital importance to have knowledge of what happens to the fetus? After all, these drugs and treatments will be used on real women in the real world whether or not we were included in the research or drug trial.

In the context of the continued struggle to legitimize the study of women's health, let us turn our attention to what should be included in an organized examination of women's health. First off, it is important to view the woman as a totality, a whole person, and not just a set of reproductive organs. The field of health education has for many years espoused a "wellness" model that serves as an excellent foundation for this discussion. The wellness concept purports that the individual must be viewed in the context of her entire life and not just her physical health. The dimensions of wellness in this model encompass social and emotional issues as well. The burgeoning field of psychoneuroimmunology calls attention to the fact that emotional states affect the functioning of the nervous and immune systems, which in turn impact one's health. Numerous studies have examined the influence of our social milieu on health and well-being. Social support is a powerful force for boosting physical health and a sense of emotional well-being. The environmental dimension of wellness encompasses much more than just toxins, bacteria, viruses and radiation. It speaks to issues like violence and substance abuse in a woman's life. Beyond the immediate environment, it also addresses the need to attack these issues on the local, state and federal levels, the larger environment.

The next dimension of wellness is intellectual wellness, the ability to think, learn and make sound judgments. As with many human faculties, the key here is "use it or lose it." Research indicates that the more intellectually active one stays, the less likely it is she will develop major cognitive problems like dementia or the less dramatic but still troublesome benign senescent forgetfulness. The final dimension of health included in the wellness model is spirituality, or, as many health scientists call it, the "s" word. In my health education classes, I have often noted that we discuss abortion, impotence and masturbation without batting an eye, yet mention spirituality and people get really uncomfortable. Still, as recent magazine and journal covers have illustrated, the medical community has begun to realize or at least reluctantly acknowledge that prayer, community, and the belief in a higher power do have an impact on lifestyle choices and health.

Keeping this wellness framework in mind, let us now proceed to a discussion of the major health issues of concern to women, beginning with mental health. It is not appropriate, nor would it be accurate, to say that women have more or fewer mental health concerns than men, but rather that their concerns are different. A five-city survey conducted by the National Institute of Mental Health (NIMH) between 1980 and 1984 found that the top three mental health issues for women are anxiety disorders, major or clinical depression, and dysthymia, or sadness. Topping the list for men was drug abuse followed by anxiety disorders and drug dependence. Before discussing the specifics, it may be helpful to discuss the nature of a psychological "disorder." To put it simply, a disorder is a condition that significantly interferes with normal daily functioning. We've all experienced sadness connected to loss, disappointment, or even hormonal changes, yet we remain able to go to school or work and do what we need to do. Clinical depression, on the other hand, is so profound a sadness that the affected individual may not even be able to get out of bed, let alone leave the house. It is the difference between stubbing your toe and breaking your leg.

With this definition in mind, let us begin by discussing anxiety disorders. The pervasive symptom of this group of disorders is extreme worry for no apparent reason. In addition, in order to be diagnosed with an anxiety disorder, one must exhibit six or more symptoms from an extensive list that includes physiological as well as psychological symptoms. In other words, it isn't just in one's head. Anxiety is felt and experienced in the body as well. The symptoms range from restlessness, muscle tension, and pounding heart to excessive fatigue and difficulty concentrating. A subset of the anxiety disorders is panic disorder. Although relatively rare as a full-blown disorder, one feature of panic disorder, the panic attack, is not so rare, especially for young women. It is estimated that at least 10% of the adult population will experience a panic episode or attack over the course of the life span. Given the amount of stress inherent in the process of higher education, it comes as no surprise that the percentage is higher among college students (12%), with college women diagnosed most frequently. What characterizes a panic attack? Often the sufferer will complain of dizziness, shortness of breath, and a feeling of impending doom. As a student of mine explained, "it is difficult to put into words the feeling that I'm going crazy, having a heart attack, or that I'm going to die." The bad news is that anxiety disorders are as prevalent as the common cold. The good news is that they respond well to treatment.

Perhaps even more relevant to a discussion of mental health issues affecting women are mood disorders. Included in this group are major or clinical depression, bipolar disorder, seasonal affective disorder, and dysthymia. Once again it is important to remember that a disorder is a condition that significantly interferes with one's life. This is an especially important distinction to remember when discussing mood disorders. Any normal human being experiences periods of sadness and low energy that subside after a while. For most of us it is not difficult to pinpoint the reason for the "blues," whether it be biological or situational. Clinical disorders, on the other hand, often appear for no clearly definable reason, and they tend to persist. As noted by a former student, "my life is wonderful. I have a great job, a loving husband and terrific kids, so why do I feel like putting a gun to my head? Not only do I feel bad, I feel guilty about feeling bad. After all, lots of people are worse off than me."

Major or clinical depression is characterized by pervasive sadness that touches every aspect of one's life. Loss of interest in activities one used to enjoy and sleep disturbances are also common. Depressed individuals often report feeling tired regardless of how much sleep they get, be it ten hours or two hours. Another common symptom is change in one's normal weight. It used to be thought that depressed people lost interest in eating and therefore lost weight, but for many clinically depressed people the opposite is true: they gain weight eating to satisfy biological and behavioral urges. Finally, difficulty in concentrating or making decisions is often present. Many sufferers of clinical depression report feeling foggy and unable to think.

No discussion of clinical depression would be complete without mentioning suicide. Many depressed individuals do think, if not talk, about committing suicide. As a matter of fact, research indicates that most "normal" individuals have thought about it at one time or another during particularly difficult periods in their lives. Talking about it will not make it happen, but ignoring it will not make it go away. Suicidal ideation, as the experts call it, is a symptom of a serious, often life-threatening disease and, as such, needs to be treated.

Not all forms of depression are at the level of major depression. Dysthymia, or generalized sadness, has similar symptoms, but to a lesser degree. Yes, female hormonal fluctuations may have something to do with the incidence of mood disorders in women. However, the literature indicates that they are more likely a result of stress caused by multiple role demands. Women are often expected to work, go to school, keep house, and take care of the spouse and kids. Increasingly, we also have to care for aging parents. If we marry the eldest son, some studies also indicate that we may end up taking care of our in-laws as well. Women still make less money for doing the same job and are subjected to violence in intimate relationships more frequently than men. Is it any wonder that women get depressed more often?

The good news about mood disorders is that they respond well to treatment: therapy, medication, and support groups. The bad news is, like treatment for addiction, women are often reluctant to seek help due to the social stigma. Women may also be prevented from seeking treatment for financial reasons, lack of childcare, and lack of accessibility.

For the last disorders considered here, the eating disorders, I will discuss obesity, anorexia and bulimia. In deference to a student of mine who recently died from complications of bulimia, I would like to say that eating disorders are not about food. Instead, they are about power, control, anger, and self-esteem. For the sake of this discussion, obesity will be defined in terms of behavior. Although there are many medical conditions which may cause or worsen obesity, it often results from a cyclic pattern of dysfunctional eating followed by guilt and despair, which triggers more dysfunctional eating. Here, I'll define dysfunctional eating as eating which occurs for reasons other than hunger: for example, when one is bored, upset, tired, or socializing.

Anorexia, or self-starvation, is characterized by intense and unrealistic fear of weight gain and refusal to maintain normal body weight. Research indicates that 90% of anorexics are women of childbearing age, many of whom cease to menstruate due to lack of appropriate caloric intake. This is turn seriously impairs present and future fertility as well as causing serious damage to every organ system in the body. Bulimia, or the "gorge-purge" syndrome, is characterized by consumption of large quantities of food (gorging) followed by vomiting (purging), use of laxatives, or over-indulgence in exercise. Once again, bulimics put incredible strain on the cardiovascular and digestive systems. Stomach acid ulcerates the esophagus, or food tube, and destroys the enamel on one's teeth. In addition, bulimics frequently suffer from hemorrhages in the eyes due to vomiting and disruption of normal bowel function from continually interrupting the digestive process.

The outcome for eating disorders is not as rosy as for mood and anxiety disorders. Talk therapy as well as medication does have a positive effect on eating disorders if one is able to get the eating-disordered client into treatment. Many sufferers do not want to change behavior and will sabotage their own recovery at every turn. Once again, the issue is control over one's life, not the food on the plate.

Considering all that can and should be said about "mental illness," the thought I would like to leave you with is this: mental illness is simply that – illness, not moral weakness. The more the public learns about the origin and treatment of mental illness, the more likely it is that the stigma will eventually disappear and women will get the help they need and deserve.

Akin to issues of mental health is an examination of addiction in women. Although men are more likely than women to abuse substances, as was previously stated, this is not meant to imply that women do not have issues with substance use, abuse, and addiction. For example, women are more likely to abuse stimulants than men are. We need to keep going. Consider the average working mother: up before the kids, packing lunches, fixing breakfast and taking care of all those last minute details before she gets herself ready for work. Then, out the door she goes to put in a full day at the office, as long as the school doesn't call to tell her one of the children is sick and needs to go home. After work, there are the endless errands: supermarket, dry cleaner, video store. Next come picking up the kids, preparing dinner, and straightening up. Finally things quiet down at around 9:00 when she gets to pay bills and catch up on the work she brought home from the office. I know this sounds like a rather traditional scenario, but the research indicates that even if she works full time, the woman still bears the brunt of the responsibility for home and children. When is the last time you heard someone comment, "I know he has a full-time job out of the home, but he's a really awful housekeeper!"

Another group of drugs utilized more frequently by women than men are opiates, or painkillers. Why do women seem to require more painkillers? It is well established that women go to the doctors more frequently and are therefore prescribed medications more often than men. Yet I am loath to believe that women are being given more painkillers because we are somehow weaker or more prone to complaint. Is it that doctors medicate women instead of dealing with the root cause of certain health issues? Is it that women are more in touch with their own anatomy and physiology and therefore know when it is appropriate to use pain-relieving medications? Is it that the average woman, once again, needs to keep going regardless of how she feels? How about all of the reasons mentioned above and a few more we may have overlooked?

Regardless of the substance being used or abused, it is notable that treatment issues also separate the sexes. In general, women are less likely to seek treatment for addiction than are men. The most prevalent theory used to explain this phenomenon deals with the social stigma. In many instances, addiction in women is seen as more of a moral issue than a health one. Women are often afraid of losing custody of their children if a substance use problem comes to light. The treatment community doesn't make the situation any easier, either. Often women are placed in mixed gender groups, which have been proven to be less effective for them. Little provision is made for childcare, flexibility of hours, or transportation to the facility. All of these factors contribute to the difficulty women experience in obtaining appropriate treatment.

Before turning to the inevitable discussion of female anatomy and physiology, the "plumbing," as I am apt to call it, I would like to mention at least some issues that the uninformed may consider to be beyond the scope of this essay: violence against women and the portrayal of women in the media. Violence has recently been identified by public health officials as a major public health issue affecting both the physical and emotional health of women and children. It is short-sighted and dangerous to consign a discussion of violence to only the political or the law enforcement arena. Domestic violence injures or kills thousands of women each year. Even if there are no visible scars, violence also erodes a woman's self esteem. I would say this has a profound effect on the health and quality of life experienced by women.

Another important issue that affects the health of women is the portrayal of women in the media. Once again, I realize I have wandered out of the traditional boundaries of health, but on second thought, perhaps not. What has a more powerful impact on how we feel about ourselves than the images that bombard us every day from television, radio, and print media? We are expected to eat, drink, smoke, and be merry, and, at the same time, stay a perfect size six. Have you ever noticed that women's magazines always seem to have the decadent chocolate cake recipe opposite the latest fad in dieting? Why is it that countries with no history of eating disorders suddenly begin to develop these problems after the introduction of American television? I contend that it is really difficult to maintain a truly balanced and healthy lifestyle in a society that has fast food joints every 50 feet. How many people do you know who grab a fast food burger on the way to the gym to work out and, once they get there, drive around for twenty minutes so they can get a parking place next to the door? Even better, have you seen the exercise fanatics who run outside every twenty minutes to smoke? It just doesn't make sense, but our society, and the way the media tells us to live, does affect our health and how we feel about ourselves.

The final part of this essay will be divided into two parts: reproductive and lifestyle issues. Lifestyle issues include dietary choices, exercise, and stress management. Although it is impossible to do an in-depth examination of any of these topics here, it may be helpful at least to hit the highlights. Nutrition is the science that explores the effects of food on the function of a living system. For women, nutritional needs revolve around age and reproductive status. During childhood the needs of both boys and girls are fairly similar; they both require sufficient calories for rapid growth and development. These needs include all the basic nutrients: carbohydrates for energy; protein for cell growth/repair; fat for hormone production, and vitamins/minerals for bone growth. Malnutrition in childhood may impact future health and fertility significantly. As important as what we eat in childhood are the food habits and attitudes we develop. I caution parents to examine their own attitudes and behaviors about food before attempting to influence the child's eating behavior. What are we telling our children via our own behaviors? Do we use food as a reward or punishment? Are we constantly dieting or bingeing? Do we as adults have a normal relationship with food? In other words, do we eat when we're hungry and stop when we're comfortable? I think I could count on one hand the number of women I know who have a healthy approach to eating and a normal relationship with food. The roots of eating disorders may well be traced back to childhood and reinforced by an appearance-obsessed media.

Adolescence continues the pattern of rapid growth and development. While it is a time of increased caloric need, it also is a time notorious for restricted eating, or dieting. How many adolescent girls do you know that are not dieting? Caloric restriction at this time may lead to problems in the development of the long bones as well as the pelvis. Caloric restriction may also lead to lower immune function and thereby increase susceptibility to disease and stress. The years prior to menopause revolve around issues of fertility. Both obesity and caloric restriction impair ovulation and thereby fertility. Also, if pregnancy is a possibility, the woman must be aware of her drug and alcohol consumption, smoking, and other health-related behaviors. Even something seemingly innocent, like caffeine consumption, may have a profound effect on fetal development. Alcohol crosses the placenta and is known to cause fetal alcohol syndrome, a condition involving both physical deformity and lowered intelligence. Nicotine from smoking crosses the placenta and is linked to low birth weight as well as asthma and other respiratory difficulties in the infant. Other families of drugs, like the stimulants, may produce a baby who is born addicted. These babies are frequently undersized, fussy, and later in life have learning and behavioral problems. Although the jury is still out on many legal and illegal substances, conventional wisdom says if you're not sure, don't use it.

Nutritional needs also differ during pregnancy and nursing. In general, the need for calories increases; however, it is not carte blanche to eat anything and everything. Once again, the nutritional integrity of the food must be considered. Malnutrition in the mother can lead to malnutrition in the fetus, which hinders growth and development and may even cause serious damage to developing organs. During pregnancy, the woman requires more protein for maintenance of her own health as well as providing raw materials for fetal growth. In addition, calcium is necessary for fetal bone growth, iron to support the mother's increase in blood volume, and, of course, folic acid for avoiding neural tube defects in the fetus. Total weight gain during pregnancy should not exceed 25-35 pounds. Obesity during pregnancy increases the risk of maternal diabetes, hypertension, kidney problems, and difficulties with labor and delivery. During the period of lactation or breast-feeding, women have a need for approximately 500 additional calories. Care must be taken in what is consumed during this period since elements of the mother's diet will be present in the breast milk. In fact, anecdotal data suggests that some infants will refuse to nurse from mothers who smoke since the taste and smell of the breast milk is affected by nicotine.

The postmenopausal years, the time of life when a woman's menstrual periods have stopped, offer a different set of nutritional challenges for women. Care must be taken to balance food intake with physical activity level in order to avoid weight gain. Bone health is also a very important issue. Without the protective effect of estrogen, women at this stage of life must be especially vigilant in consuming sufficient calcium. Lack of sufficient calcium in the diet can lead to osteoporosis, which in turn increases the risk of painful bone fractures and breaks. Beyond the pain and cost of treatment, skeletal problems can seriously limit a woman's mobility and, thereby, her independence.

The second "lifestyle issue" to be discussed here is exercise. As I tell my health classes, if ever there were a fountain of youth and an ongoing source of health and vitality, it is exercise. If only it came in a bottle! The physical benefits of exercise are well known. Exercise boosts the metabolism, allowing the body to utilize calories more effectively. Exercise also improves heart and lung function. It has been shown to decrease the risk of adult onset (type 2) diabetes, osteoporosis, and certain types of cancer. Perhaps less tangible but equally important are the psychological benefits of exercise: research indicates that exercise also modifies mood. It can be a powerful ally in the treatment of depression and other mood disorders. Research also indicates that regular exercise can help alleviate the physical and emotional symptoms of Premenstrual Syndrome.

Once again, historically, most of the studies exploring the benefits of exercise have been conducted on male subjects. Happily, this situation is changing. For example, it has been shown that exercise helps to strengthen the pelvic muscles aiding in childbirth and helping to prevent incontinence later in life. Although there is still much controversy surrounding how much exercise and what type is most beneficial, most experts agree that any sensible exercise program should include both aerobic activity and strength training or muscle building activity. Aerobic activity includes any activity that increases the heart rate to the zone between 60% and 80% of one's target heart rate. In case you're curious, a quick and dirty target heart rate can be calculated by subtracting one's age from 220, then multiplying by .6 and .8 respectively. Aerobic activity should take place for 20 minutes at least 3 times per week. Strength training is exactly what the name suggests: activity that works and thereby strengthens the major muscle groups. Strength training sessions should occur approximately three times per week with a day rest period in between working any particular muscle group to avoid injury. Strength training builds metabolically active tissue that in turn helps the individual avoid weight gain. In other words, you build muscle to burn fat. Not only does exercise help people avoid weight gain, but any woman over 40 will attest to the fact that weight maintenance, never mind weight loss, is virtually impossible without exercise. In short, exercise is vital in helping one look good, feel good, and function well. A word of caution is necessary, however, for those individuals who tend to overindulge in exercise. Excessive exercise can result in damage to joints, muscle, and soft tissue. Too much exercise can also disrupt a woman's normal menstrual cycle and impair fertility. Over-exercise also has been linked to eating disorders. Both anorexics and bulimics may abuse exercise in the quest for the perfect body. More is not always better, and something that is beneficial in measured doses may in fact be extremely harmful if overused.

I have purposely postponed the discussion of reproduction to the end, not because it is the least important issue in this essay, but rather because it is frequently considered the only issue of importance in woman's health. As discussed in the beginning of this essay, women have been excluded from research and drug trials because of their reproductive anatomy and physiology. Is it any wonder that the majority of women are offended by being classified in such a narrow and erroneous fashion? Although I will refrain from turning this into a biology lesson, I will begin this discussion by advocating the benefits of education. Every woman needs to be aware of her reproductive anatomy and physiology, or what her body looks like and how it functions. How can a woman tell if there is a problem if she is unaware of what is normal for her? Also, how can she communicate with her health care practitioner if she doesn't know the proper names for anatomical structures? Having problems "down there" with my "thingy" is not a very constructive way to begin a discussion with one's physician. Also, it puts the woman in an inferior position in terms of the doctor-patient relationship. Instead of the ideal circumstance in which both doctor and patient work cooperatively towards the goal of good health, an uninformed patient gives the physician total control over her health and well-being while abrogating her own responsibility. Research indicates that the quality of the doctor-patient relationship is key in determining whether or not a patient will adhere to the physician's recommendations and thereby get well. If you do not feel comfortable with your health care provider, go the extra mile and find someone who does inspire confidence, someone who will work with you and not on you.

No discussion of woman's health would be complete without some mention of fertility and contraception. Regarding contraception, let me begin by saying once again that it is vital for a woman to educate herself about all options available to her. I realize that issues concerning pregnancy and its prevention are controversial. As a health educator, I feel ethically compelled to make sure my students are provided with accurate and current information. Beyond that, I believe each individual woman is capable of making reproductive decisions in the context of her moral, cultural, and religious background.

If a woman opts to control her fertility, there are several factors to be considered. How costly is the method, and can she easily afford it? How reliable is the method in preventing pregnancy? Does the method protect her from sexually transmitted infections?

Finally, how does the method mesh with her lifestyle? In other words, if she is only sexually active occasionally, does she want to take a pill every day? In terms of pregnancy prevention, there are chemical methods which inhibit ovulation and change the integrity of the uterine lining. Barrier methods, which prevent egg and sperm from uniting, also are readily available. Then there is female sterilization, or the tubal ligation, a permanent method of birth control that closes off the fallopian tubes and prevents the egg from reaching the uterus. Natural family planning, or what I like to call fertility awareness, is also an option. If one is trying to avoid pregnancy, or get pregnant, for that matter, it is absolutely essential that she understands and charts her menstrual cycle. For a normal 28-day cycle, ovulation, or the release of the egg from the ovary, occurs mid-cycle, around day 14. Since sperm can live in the female reproductive tract for a few days, it is important that intercourse be avoided for about four days before and four days after ovulation. Around the time of ovulation, the cervical mucous becomes thin and stringy to allow for the passage of sperm to the egg. The woman's resting body temperature also spikes at ovulation. Although I do not intend this to be a "how to" manual for natural family planning, I do wish to make the point that in order for this method to have a chance at preventing pregnancy, the woman must know what is going on with her body. She also should know that this method is not all that reliable.

Finally, I should also mention that abstinence is certainly an option worthy of consideration. In my zeal to provide women with information about their options, I sometimes forget that a woman may freely choose not to be sexually active. If this decision is made for moral, religious or health reasons, then I applaud it. If this decision is made out of fear or ignorance, then I believe it is harmful to the woman, her family, and ultimately society at large.

My final task is to pull the pieces together and leave you, the reader, with a sense of the importance of studying women's health. Actually, I hope to leave you with much more. I hope you walk away angry about the exclusion of women from the research as well as the other inequities and injustices women must overcome in the quest for good health and a respectable quality of life. I also hope that you caught on to the underlying theme of education and personal responsibility. If you are not committed to your own health and well-being, why should anyone else be? If you do not seek to educate yourself on the issues, don't be surprised if society doesn't either. Societal change begins with individual commitment. Each and every woman should and must be an advocate for her own health. Spread the word.

# Caught Between Homophobia and Peer Pressure: A Classroom Experiment

## by Teresa Bevin

When I presented a standard exercise on homosexuality to a group dynamics class in which female students were coincidentally in the majority, I did not expect anything more than a standard, almost predictable outcome. Alternative lifestyles produce responses as diverse as my student population, but the issue of how peer pressure influences their reactions deserves deeper exploration, as the following experiment demonstrates.

We have entered a new millennium and are experiencing increased exposure to gay themes, noteworthy and not, in films, television programs, books, and other media. But in spite of the exposure, and the small but vocal number of entertainment celebrities and sports heroes who have declared themselves gay or lesbian, widespread ignorance about homosexual lifestyles prevails in our society.

The gay and lesbian movement undergoes a metamorphosis with each new generation. Young gays and lesbians step out onto the seemingly firmer land tread by the previous generation of gays and lesbians in their struggles for rights, visibility, and validation. With each decade, it seems that gays are "coming out" at an earlier age. Teenagers and young adults today are more likely to gather the strength to face their parents with their personal truth than those of ten years ago. More are able to make it to "the other side" relatively unharmed. In the nineties the index of young homosexuals who found it necessary to leave their parental home upon disclosure of their sexual orientation showed a marked decrease as compared with those of the eighties. Nonetheless, most heterosexuals who have little or indirect contact with open homosexuals still tend to believe that all gay men and lesbians lead one kind of lifestyle—one that revolves around sex and little else. Therein the overused comment by those who want to talk themselves into a position of open-mindedness: "I have nothing against gays as long as they don't come on to me."

Another residual belief is that among gay and lesbian couples, one partner must "play" the male, the other the female, and that this role reversal is reflected in the gender-distorting dress, gestures, and speech gays "typically" adopt. The unknowing do not realize that many gay people are seldom identified as such while in their everyday roles of the banker, the teacher, and physician with whom they come in contact.

I am dumbfounded by the lack of understanding and acceptance among the general heterosexual population, regardless of their age, level of education, or cultural background. Despite what appears as growing awareness of the subject and increasing support among law-makers and organizations, how is it possible that we are still in the dark as far as the acceptance of gay and lesbian lifestyles? Is it possible that the vilification of a minority is almost as strong today as it was twenty years ago? Though evidence supports my observations, I still hope for substantial changes any day now.

With these factors in mind, I make attempts to bring forth a degree of understanding about homosexuals as well as other social minorities to my students of psychology and mental health. My focus is on helping students know and feel the difference between tolerance and acceptance.

Two years ago I decided to try an exercise suggested by John R. Suler, Ph.D. (1995), of the Department of Psychology of Rider University in New Jersey for the discussion on homosexuality in my group dynamics class. The goal of the exercise is to uncover the different views group members may have about the subject of homosexual lifestyles, and to spark a lively exchange among them. This kind of discussion often brings an element of understanding among some students, though in this instance, not as many as I had expected.

Although students who are interested in a career in the field of mental health tend to be more open to a variety of lifestyles, the issue of homosexuality inevitably brings out the best and the worst from almost any group. This time I was in for a surprise, or rather, two surprises.

## The Exercise

I divided the large group into six groups of three students each. I aimed to balance the small groups as much as possible in terms of age, gender, ethnicity, temperament and experience, but especially temperament. There was at least one of the more outspoken students per group, and one male in each of five groups, since there weren't enough male students in the class for the six groups.

My instructions to the students were to listen carefully as I read several statements aloud. Once a statement was read, they were to discuss it among themselves in their small group, then vote and reach a consensus as to whether they agreed or disagreed with the statement. When all groups indicated they had reached an agreement or were unable to do so, a new statement was read. After all the statements were read and all the votes were counted, the entire group turned to face each other in a larger circle to discuss the exercise.

The statements read, in sequence, were:

- Homosexuality is normal.
- Having a homosexual friend is acceptable to me.
- Having homosexual neighbors is acceptable to me.
- Children's books should portray more homosexual parents.
- Homosexuals should be allowed in military service.
- Homosexuals should be able to form legal unions.
- Committed homosexual couples should receive all of the legal benefits of marriage.
- It is acceptable for homosexuals to raise children.
- It is acceptable to me if my child's teacher is a homosexual.
- I would vote for a homosexual who was running for president.
- It is acceptable to me if one or more of my children turned out to be homosexual.

- It is acceptable to me if I found out that one of my parents was homosexual.

My first surprise came when few students showed any significant reaction to any of the statement, and most of the small groups essentially agreed with the statements. All five male students expressed complete acceptance toward homosexuals. Two African-born women over the age of thirty-five, and one twenty-two-year-old Latin-American woman were the only group members who registered initial objections around the issue of homosexuals teaching or raising children, but were quickly swayed to agree with their focus group. One of the African women objected to the very last statement, saying that if she ever found out that her mother was a lesbian, she could never forgive her. She faced strong criticism from other group members, and she too chose to agree with the statement, though it was obvious that she did so under pressure from her peers. It was my expectation that the diversity in the class would have some bearing on the final results of the exercise as the perception of gays and lesbians in other nations varies widely. Although the United States is not the best place for gays, it is not the worst either. And while the European community generally discourages discrimination against gays on every front, many underdeveloped countries still maintain little less than a policy of genocide against homosexuals.

The exercise, contrary to my expectations, provoked only a short period of discussion during which group members adamantly proclaimed themselves as very accepting of homosexuality, though not one student revealed himself or herself as homosexual. There was no need for me, as has been the case with other classes, to stress the difference between acceptance and tolerance to an already accepting group of people who aspire to be professional helpers and group leaders. I was happy to discover that this class had developed further than any previous group. I was excited to discover a new degree of openness, and my heart was filled with gratitude for the evident change. Finally, I thought, enlightenment is here. The new generations will carry the torch of acceptance.

Unaccustomed as I was to such a smooth culmination of a discussion dealing with the topic of homosexuality, I decided to take the exercise a bit further. If the students were so progressive, they might as well look at the issue from another angle. With the students seated in a wide circle, I asked the following questions (Jennings, 1994) while making sure there was enough time in between questions for spontaneous reactions.

- What do you think caused your heterosexuality?
- When and how did you decide you were heterosexual?
- Is it possible that heterosexuality is a phase you will grow out of?
- Is it possible you are heterosexual because you fear the same sex?
- If you have never slept with someone of the same sex, how do you know you wouldn't prefer that? Is it possible that all you need is a good gay experience?
- With whom have you discussed your heterosexuality, and how did they react?
- Heterosexuality is not offensive as long as you leave others alone. Why, however, do so many heterosexuals try to seduce others into their orientation?
- Most child molesters are heterosexual. Do you consider it safe to expose your children to heterosexuals? Heterosexual teachers, particularly?
- Why do heterosexuals make such spectacles of their heterosexuality by kissing and hugging in public?
- Given the problems heterosexuals face, would you consider aversion therapy to try to change them?

The students' incredulous reaction to these questions was to be expected. But in spite of their amusement, some of them indicated that they probably would think about the exercise for a long time to come, and that was enough for me.

My second surprise came over one month later when toward the end of the semester, I gave the class a take-home final exam. The students were asked to write about the dynamics they had observed in class throughout the semester, and to discuss their individual role in those dynamics. The last part of the exam was a self-evaluation that consisted of ten questions, one of which required that the student discuss the one group exercise that was most uncomfortable for him or her, or one in which they wished they had done or said something other than what they actually did or said. I was shocked to find that over a third of the class, all women, had chosen the exercise on homosexuality as the one that had produced the most discomfort for them. There it was, in black and white, one student after the other said that she regretted not having spoken about her true feelings on the issue, mainly because she feared ridicule and rejection from her classmates. One African-American student cited biblical scriptures to convince me of the sinful, unnatural character of homosexuality. She went so far as to reprimand me for bringing up the subject in class, because she had paid so much money for the course and that was not a topic she cared to discuss or to learn about. She had grown up within "a normal family" where nobody ever thought of behaving in such a "perverted" manner. She stated that none of her children would ever turn out to be homosexual because she would raise them in a proper, "normal" environment where those things would not happen. In addition, she wrote that if she had known what the class was about beforehand, she would have not signed up for it. In contrast, one of the African-born women who, during the exercise, expressed objections to the idea of homosexuals teaching or raising children, wrote that she had changed her mind as a result of the second part of the exercise when I asked the group about their heterosexuality. She stated that she could now accept, without reservations, the idea that homosexuals are not focused exclusively on the issue of sex and deserve the same considerations as heterosexuals. Another student said she felt very uncomfortable about the issue of homosexuality because her own mother had "turned into a lesbian" after the age of forty. She no longer felt free to introduce her mother to her friends because she felt they would all know what her orientation was just by looking at her, and she stood to lose friends over it.

Two young women, one Caucasian and one Asian-American wrote that they believed themselves to have lesbian tendencies and that they were denying and fighting these tendencies in order to fit into a homophobic society. One of them wrote that she wanted to have children and did not think that children deserved to grow up with two mothers and no father, or with one single lesbian mother. The fact that she knew that a number of her classmates were heterosexual single mothers with healthy children apparently had no impact on her outlook. Both young women expressed confidence in their decision to live a successful, straight life, though they knew sometimes their feelings might betray them. One of them stressed that she was willing and able to control herself her entire life if necessary. Other students of diverse backgrounds, though all female, stated that they could give counsel to homosexuals because they "had nothing against them," but that they would never believe that homosexuality was simply a matter of sexual orientation, but a choice, and that anyone could change those desires in order to live a "normal" life without judgment or ridicule from mainstream society.

I was flabbergasted by the unexpected responses. If so many students had such strong reactions, why did they choose not to speak up during the exercise? Where had I gone wrong? Had I made my own feelings on the subject so clear that I had intimidated them into silence? Filled with self-doubt, I asked myself many questions. But as my shock wore off, I realized that although the exercise had not provoked a lengthy discussion as it was designed to do, it worked perfectly as a gauge of the students' feelings about homosexuality and homosexual lifestyles, and it had produced the most extraordinary results. The exercise had made them all think. In perspective, the number of students who actually condemned homosexuality was very low (5 out of 18), and in the face of so much acceptance they had decided to keep quiet about their true feelings. This was quite different from my past experiences while teaching group dynamics, when those who did not approve of homosexual lifestyles were often in the dominant majority, and could easily drown out the opinions of the minority. Historically, the most passionate opposition to homosexual lifestyles had usually come from male students. Now the most prejudiced students were females who, knowing themselves in the homophobic minority, had preferred to remain silent than to be seen as bigots by the majority of the group. Had the tables turned? Had some group members been caught between homophobia and peer pressure?

But what about the students who chose to remain silent? Had they missed an opportunity to learn through discussion for fear of the repercussions, or had the learning taken place anyway, by default? Was it all because so many women, in their desire to please and be accepted, often avoid voicing disagreement when they perceive the majority may be against them? Perhaps the current media trend on the subject of homosexuality has contributed to an atmosphere in which gay is "cool," even fashionable, and opposing it is not, and the results of the exercise reflected this and nothing more. Perhaps the time has come when larger numbers of people are learning to perceive human contrasts as examples of diversity, instead of seeing them as barriers to interpersonal communication and understanding.

What about the fact that the segment most disturbed by the issue of homosexuality were the female students? The answer may lie in what those women had in common. They all had lived on or below the poverty line at some point in the not-too-distant past, and not only in the United States, but also in Haiti, Nigeria and Peru, where the poverty line is much lower. They were either single mothers themselves or their mothers were, and they held very strong religious beliefs. In contrast, the similarly culturally diverse male students had never been married, all came from middle-class families, and their freedom of choice was clearly greater than that of the prejudiced women. The men's exposure to differences had been greater, as was their feeling of personal freedom. Those who do not see themselves as free are more likely to be opposed to the freedoms of others, since whether real or perceived, lack of freedom breeds feelings of vulnerability and fear of the unknown.

This exercise left me with more questions than answers, but sometimes the questions are far more significant than the answers because of the thoughts they promote and stimulate. The next time I employ this exercise in class, I will be ready to challenge any apparent implicit acceptance of homosexuality, and I will not see this exercise as one that will provoke discussion on its own, without persistent probing.

At the dawn of the millennium we still have a long way to go. But somehow, steps are being taken and minds are changing. Sometimes changes present themselves in the most unusual and paradoxical ways, and we may need to look for nuggets of hope among immovable boulders of prejudice. Perhaps just the knowledge that a person's prejudice often stems from her own oppression is the nugget that will cause the boulder to shift.

# References

Jennings, K. (Ed.). (1994). Becoming visible: A reader in gay and lesbian history for high school and college students (pp. 25-26). Los Angeles: Allyson Publications.

Suler, J. R. (1995). Teaching clinical psychology. On-line document. <http//www.rider.edu/users/suler/tcp.html>.

# Women in Front of and Behind the Camera
by Robert L. Giron

## Introduction

Perhaps no other medium has had a greater impact on our lives than film, and so when one approaches the topic of women in film, one is faced with a plethora of information which can only be superficially discussed in a chapter on such a vast subject matter. To this end, I have decided to focus on the images of women in film over the years as projected by men in contrast to those images of women in film as projected by women. These varied portrayals touch on themes that are often repeated in film, from gender identification to issues of skin color, as defined by ethnicity or nationality, and the polarity between the opposites within these perimeters. It is essential that one keep an open mind while delving into this topic as these images are fluid and are not always exclusive to the particular gender of the director nor are they always lineal in role development. Indeed I have found that some of the images overlap, however, the attitudes the directors intended or which reflect the expectations or mores of a particular time are often quite intentional.

I feel the need to briefly touch on an important point that E. Ann Kaplan makes in her seminal book *Feminism & Film* before examining this topic: "A feminist perspective should not be confused with the literal gender of the scholar: males can write feminist criticism, and women can write criticism that is not feminist" (1). Certainly mythology has had a great effect on people's live and literature and what quickly comes to mind are the woes of Eve and Pandora, for example. Women as well as men have kept mythologies alive and part of cultural traditions such that one should not be surprised to see similar mythologies or themes which have converged over the years and have been transformed by men and women in film, though with varying effects.

## Discussion

Taking into account the power of mythology perhaps more so than history itself, mentioning the Greek myth of Pandora's Box is merited. Laura Mulvey states in her article *The Myth of Pandora: A Psychoanalytical Approach*, "Pandora, from a feminist perspective, has to be conceived as a puzzle or riddle in which the spatial division is part of a cipher. If the metaphor of unveiling a concealed truth is applied to the Pandora myth, it necessarily stays stuck within the spatial terms of the myth. It is essential for feminists to analyze through metaphors of understanding as 'deciphering' rather than metaphors of understanding as 'seeing'" (in Pietropaola 3-4). Although the myth of opening Pandora's Box has been used repeated to convey releasing calamities into the world, what is needed as Mulvey states is to "decode, articulate, and analyze these symptoms in order to transform the look of curiosity, the desire to know, into understanding so that the status of the female body as signifier can be challenged and transformed" (in Pietropaola 18). Unfortunately, the female body has been represented in so many varying ways that to generalize would be fruitless, though patterns are apparent.

To delve into the male v. female struggle rooted in Freud's theories is necessary because as Kaplan has so eloquently discussed its projection onto screens "…psychoanalysts agree that, for whatever reason—the fear of castration (Freud), or the attempt to deny the existence of the sinister female genital (Horney)—men endeavor to find the penis in women. Feminist film critics have seen this phenomenon (clinically known as fetishism) operating in the cinema; the camera (unconsciously) fetishizes the female form, rendering it phallus-like so as to mitigate woman's threat. Men [according to Laura Mulvey], that is, turn 'the represented figure itself into a fetish so that it becomes reassuring rather than dangerous' (hence overvaluation, the cult of the female star) (121). Instead, perhaps men perceive women who are assertive if not aggressive as man-like or phallus-like and within this frame of mind men are able to deal with the women as equals, and given that men often enjoy physical if not mental combat between equals such women are perceived as a reliable challenge within the male context. In other words, with women as quasi equals, men are more comfortable dealing with them within the male context, for non-phallus-like or vaginal beings are not easily understood and are more of a threat because one cannot predict what they will do nor can one deal with them as *men*.

The role of women in film has its beginning in the silent film era, but fortunately men as well as women shaped this early form of the medium. In its early stage, the financial pay dirt of film was not yet known and so women were able to enter the field beside men; however, as the Hollywood film moguls cultivated the financial interest in film, women slowly saw their role diminish as directors.

In discussing women in film, no doubt many know of or perhaps have seen indelible images that have become American icons of film. Lillian Gish's role in "True Heart Susie" (1919) as the pure woman who is in love with her neighbor and makes sacrifices for him as directed by D. W. Griffith is in direct contrast to Jerome Storm's *The Vamp* (1918) in which Enid Bennett plays the role of Nancy who uses her seductiveness to "vamp" her man whom she later marries. As the silent films developed into "talkies," women continued to play a variety of roles from Marlene Dietrich, an unknown actress at the time, in *Der Blaue Engel* (1930) as a cabaret dancer by night at the Blue Angel, where she sings her now famous throaty version of "Falling in Love Again,"and a sexually charged teacher by day in a boy's prep school. But in *Morocco* (1930) also directed by Josef von Sternberg, Dietrich seductively dressed in a tux flirts with a woman in the club and seals the flirtation with a kiss, effectively touching on the ambiguity of sexuality and still keeps her femininity intact. This simply act of females kissing will continue to resonant for years in the mind's of men and women alike.

Certainly Marlene Dietrich and Mae West among others have attracted the attention of numerous scholars for their provocative roles which often walk on the fine line of gender-bending, though in different ways. However, "feminist film studies has extended its analysis of gender in film to interrogate the representation of race, class, sexuality, and nation; encompassed media such as television and video into its paradigms; and contributed to the rethinking of film historiography, most notably in relation to consumer culture" (White in Hill 117).

It is crucial to mention Mae West's impact on film and culture in general, for as a sex symbol she not only played roles given to her but she also created her own image as an active screenwriter. A pro with double entendres, she was able to dazzle the censors with humor to the point that she was able to get away with salacious comments by today's standards of politically correctness by pundits who are attempting to puritanize our language and actions. It is also significant to mention that West was quite aware that she was clearly the Queen of the Gays, such that West for years was the premier choice of female impersonators. West said that gay actors became her sisters; 'They were all crazy about me and my costumes. They were the first ones to imitate me in my presence' (as quoted in Braun 51).

There are countless others that warrant mentioning but along with West and Dietrich many played the seductive woman, the good woman, and the bad woman. Instead what attracts my attention is the role of Rosaura Revueltas as Esperanza (Hope) in *Salt of the Earth* (1954) by the blacklisted director Herbert J. Biberman. In this tale set in New Mexico the male workers are up against the Anglo bosses who are prejudice and resist the unionization. Not so surprisingly, Revueltas in a "macho" world along with her fellow women folk take over the strike and conquer the moment so that the men get their just reward, thereby the women become the salt of the earth of their community. "When students see this film they are shocked at the boldest of the *cinema vérité* that bites with truth. For even today some of these very issues are still being fought in our society" (Giron 41). In a like manner, Sally Field in her Oscar-winning role in *Norma Rae* (1979) directed by Martin Ritt organizes workers in her Southern community and becomes the "hero" much like Julia Roberts who plays the lead role in *Erin Brockovich* (2000) directed by Steven Soderberg.

The portrayal of gender-bending whether for comic relief or for male enjoyment in terms of the male challenge context has been repeated numerous times. Julie Andrews in *Victor/Victoria* (1982) takes Blake Edwards' gender twist to a hilarious level of perfection when she states, "You want me to be a woman pretending to be a man pretending to be a woman?" This film merits our attention because although a comedy it aptly depicts cultural expectations with regard to gender roles, be they right or wrong, and the worn battle of the sexes. Of course, one needs to mention Barbra Steisand's debut as a director with *Yentl* (1983), which also challenged cultural as well as religious norms in a cross-dressing gender-bender, with echoes of *Queen Cristina* (1933), with Greta Garbo who played a Hollywood remake of Queen Cristina, made into a heterosexual, who was in reality a lesbian (Darren 173). In like manner, director Sally Potter adapted Virginia Woolf's novel from 1928 into an androgynous Orlando played by Tilda Swinton who captivates Queen Elizabeth I, regally played to the hilt by gay actor Quentin Crisp (Murray 461). To try to explain the gender twists by saying that some people manifest bisexual tendencies would be too simplistic. Instead both the physical attraction to these gender-bending characters and the psychological shock to one's sexuality continues to succeed because it takes the viewer to places he/she is afraid to travel to, whereas watching a character in film is perceived as save, even if one identifies with the character, because no one else will ever know this personal secret.

The study of women in film as already mentioned is quite vast and since the feminist movement this area of study has mushroomed into a field of study unto its own. As Judith Mayne states, "First, women's cinema refers to films made by women, and by women *directors* for the most part (as opposed, say, to screenwriters or actresses)" (2). The foremost American female Hollywood director is Dorothy Arzner whose most noted films include *Blood and Sand* (1922), *The Wild Party* (1929), and *Craig's Wife* (1936) and a close second is Ida Lupino *Not Wanted* (1949), *The Bigamist* (1953), and numerous TV series from *Alfred Hitchcock Presents* (1955) to Thriller (1960) to *The Ghost and Mrs.* Muir (1968). More recent directors include Claudia Weill *Girlfriends* (1978) and Amy Heckerling *Fast Times at Ridgemont High* (1982) and *Johnny Dangerously* (1984), *Look Who's Talking* (1989), *and Clueless* (1995). One also needs to mention several European female directors, such as Leni Riefenstahl *The Olympiad* (USA 1938), even if current feminists would rather not include her, or Lina Wertmüller *When Women Had Tails* (USA 1970), *When Women Lost Their Tails* (USA 1972), *Seven Beauties* (USA 1976), and *Sotto...sotto* (USA 1984). Contemporary directors who have left their mark include Chantal Akerman *Je, tu, il, elle* (1974) and *Seven Women, Seven Sins* (USA 1986); Helke Sander *Love Is the Beginning of All Terrors* (1984); independent documentary filmmaker Connie Field *The Life and Times of Rosie the Riveter* (*1980*); Michelle Parkerson *Stormé: Lady of the Jewel Box* (1991); and avant-garde independents Michelle Citron *Daughter Rite* (1979) and Sally Potter *The Gold Diggers* (1983), *I Am an Ox, I Am a Horse, I Am a Man, I Am a Woman* (1988), and *Orlando* (1992).

The variety and diversity that these films represent complicate the task of trying to define or characterize what 'women cinema' is today, but many films deal with gender-bending and the cultural struggle women have in male-dominated societies. When one examines the films directed by non-whites, issues of ethnicity and skin color play a major role in addition to those already mentioned.

Interestingly, six of the twelve female directors mentioned in the previous paragraph are European which perhaps speaks to the difficulties women have had in the USA to break into the film industry, aside from the early stages of the film industry when men had not taken the financial potential of the industry seriously. However, one should not make the assumption that directing abroad was or is any easier for women than in the USA. It is noteworthy to mention that in France "From all major filmmaking roles, women were effectively excluded. This contrasts to some extent with the preclassic cinema, where female directors such as Germaine Dulac and Marguerite Duras, Nina Companeez and Agnès Varda could play leading roles" (Crisp 207). Nonetheless, these directors have left a lasting impact on other directors.

Given that the film industry cultivated a psychological craving for film, it is not surprising that Hollywood eventually has produced films that are intended for female viewers. Molly Haskell rather shockingly explains the import of the 'woman's film':

> At the lowest level, as soap opera, the 'woman's film' fills a masturbatory need, it is soft-core emotional porn for the frustrated housewife. The weepies are founded on a mock-Aristotelian and politically conservative aesthetic whereby women spectators are moved, not by pity and fear but by self-pity and tears, to accept, rather than reject, their lot. That there should be a need and an audience for such an opiate suggests an unholy amount of real misery (155).

The other aspect of woman's film is the fascination with the sexuality of women, both from the heterosexual as well as the homosexual point of view. To this end, Dorothy Arzner, the first female to join the Directors Guild of America, stands as a maverick in the film industry, and as a lesbian she was often thought of as 'one of the men.' "Arzner has served as an important example of a woman director working within the Hollywood system who managed, in however limited ways, to make films that disturb the conventions of Hollywood narrative" (Mayne 98). Surprisingly Arzner's film *The Wild Party* (1929) "touches on lesbian relationships" though she accomplished this in a very subtle manner (Bryant 14). Arzner who worked with Katharine Hepburn in *Christopher Strong* (1933) was able to portray Hepburn in men's clothes as an "aviatrix who falls in love with an older, married man" (Mayne 99) much to the dismay of the audience of the times. Arzner steps into the arena of female relationships with the film *Craig's Wife* (1936); however, as Mayne points out:

> To be sure, there is much 'female bonding'—to use the preferred phrase whereby lesbianism is usually repressed—in Arzner's films, but that female bonding takes many forms, one of which is lesbian; and it is the lesbian inflection where Arzner's authorial signature is most in evidence. Second, lesbianism raises some crucial questions concerning identification and desire in the cinema, questions with particular relevance to female cinematic authorship. Cinemaoffers simultaneous affirmation and dissolution of the binary oppositions upon which our most fundamental notions of self and other are based. In feminist film theory, one of the most basic working assumptions has been that in the classical cinema, at least, there is a fit between the hierarchies of masculinity and femininity on the one hand, and activity and passivity on the other. If disrupting and disturbing that fit is a major task for filmmakers and theorists, then lesbianism would seem to have a strategically important function. For one of the 'problems' that lesbianism poses, insofar as representation is concerned, is precisely the fit between the paradigms of sex and agency, the alignment of masculinity with activity and femininity with passivity (117-118).

There have been numerous films in which lesbians have been portrayed negatively, however, Woody Allen's *Manhattan* (1979) offered a "*positive* image of lesbianism in the character of Jill (Meryl Streep): she is attractive, confident, in a successful relationship, and does not come to a tragic end" (Weiss 58) unlike the characters in *The Fox* (1968), directed by Mark Rydell, or *The Killing of Sister George* (1968), directed by Robert Aldrich. Much has been written about the film *The Hunger* (1980), directed by Tony Scott, in which Catherine Deneuve's character, a vampire, seduces the butch character Susan Sarandon plays. However, Theda Bara who played a vampire in the film *Sin* (1915) stated "Women are my greatest fans because they see in my [role as] vampire the impersonal vengeance of all their unavenged wrongs...I have the face of a vampire, perhaps, but the heart of a femisiste" (as quoted in Weiss). "In the first decade of the cinema there were at least forty films about this mortal female vampire, whom men could find sexually enticing while women could fantasize female empowerment"(Weiss 98). The vampire portrayal plays into the gender-bending theme from a different angle. That is, a beautiful women, i.e., French actress Catherine Deneuve, and the mysterious if not exotic woman, i.e., Jewish actress Theda Bara, are able to transcend normalcy and entice both men and women in a highly homoerotic manner whereby the viewer is both aroused and challenged.

Certainly one cannot assume that everyone perceives such films in the same light just as one must not assume that women think the same or have the same objectives, one must also not assume that all homosexuals think the same or have the same objectives. And although many women filmmakers have been or are lesbian, one must not assume that all women filmmakers are lesbian. Certainly, Pratibha Parmar, a lesbian Kenyan-born Indian Black British activist, has been most vocal in making her goals known with regard to identify of politics and the politics of race as they relate to lesbianism. In her own words, Parmar explains:

> One of my concerns as a filmmaker is to challenge the normalizing and universalizing tendencies within the predominantly white lesbian and gay communities—to assert the diversity of cultural and racial identities within the umbrella category of gay and lesbian. There is a need also to redefine 'community,' and just as there isn't a homogenous Black community, similarly there isn't a monolithic lesbian and gay community (9).

Another twist to gender-bending can be found in films by men and women that include men taking on roles usually performed by women, such as parenting. Male directors first began to introduce men taking care of children in such films as *Kramer v.*

*Kramer* (1979), directed by Robert Benton, *Three Men and a Baby* (1987), directed by Leonard Nimoy, and *Raising Arizona* (1987), directed by Joel Coen. Eventually, Amy Heckerling would take this topic on in her successful film *Look Who's Talking* (1989); however, as Lucinda Joy Peach states "there are no data showing that large numbers of fathers are, in fact, fulfilled by making child care the center of their lives" (246). But with many families becoming two-wage earners in order to support the average household, males/fathers culturally appear to be taking on more household/parenting duties than has been the traditional norm. So what seems to be happening is that both the cultural norms are reflected in films and films in turn affect the cultural expectations in much the same way women in the 1920s imitated what was projected onto the screen.

Skin color has also been an issue in film about women as nonwhite or minority women have traditionally been portrayed as servants or members of the under class. So Julie Dash's short film *Illusions* (1942) about a light-skinned black woman who passes as white and who works herself up from a secretary to the administrative level at National Studios was daring for its time (Mayne 59). Hollywood eventually began to include black people in films as requested by the National Association for the Advancement of Colored People but not always in a good light. In 1959 the film *Imitation of Life* echoed the theme from *Illusions* but this time a black housekeeper's daughter tries to pass as white. Unfortunately, Hollywood did not treat other non-Anglo/non-white men or women any better for years to come.

Regrettably many earlier films by black women often have been overlooked by a predominantly white industry. However, as early as 1927, Lita Lawrence made her mark with her film *Motherhood: Life's Greatest Miracle,* and recently discovered ethnographic short films by author Zora Heal Hurston from the 1920s have come to light. But many filmmakers, both male and female, have had "their work ignored and/or poorly distributed, to some extent [due to the] critical crisis of representation. One response has been the formation of independent filmmaking collectives such as The Sankofa Film and Video Collective" (Foster 4). But most film critics generally overlook the independent films of African-American and Asian-American women but they promote the films of Spike

Lee and Robert Townsend as well as other non-white men. Indeed these women "challenge dominant cinema, which is predominantly white, Eurocentric, and male dominated. Nevertheless, they resist and disrupt racism, sexism, and homophobia, which are ever-present in most world cinema" (Foster 3).

One would hope that the state of independent filmmakers might improve in the future but the film industry has become such a costly endeavor from salaries for all involved to distribution that realistically the future is bleak. For one the National Endowments of the Arts and Humanities have been cut and producers are not too anxious to risk their investments on projects that cannot deliver to the masses which in turn produce millions of dollars in profits. What this means is that the Hollywood effect has taken hold and profits not style or message are the goal of most producers and filmmakers. As a result, independents have turned to European and independent film festivals to premier their work. In this manner, Julie Dash showed her film *Daughters of the Dust* (1990) at the Sundance Film Festival, which was awarded Best Cinematography (Klotman 122), in Utah and later in Munich, Germany to much acclaim. Then after having been told by white Hollywood male producers that there was not a market for her film, in 1991 Kino International of New York took on the distribution of *Daughters of the Dust*, thereby making Dash the first African-American woman filmmaker to have a film released in the USA (Foster 49). Of course, this could not have been possible if the film had not been well received, but Dash found an audience willing to take her work seriously.

In 1993, Parmar's documentary *Warrior Masks* which was produced by author Alice Walker and based on her novel *Possessing the Secret of Joy* created quite a stir. Walker interviewed several women from African countries and even in England who either experienced female genital mutilation or who perform the ritual. Much to the distress of Walker and Parmar, many of the women were unable or refused "to question such a thoroughly misogynist tradition" and "Parmar and Walker insist that all women rethink racist and misogynist 'cultural practices' that brutalize women on a daily basis" (Foster 91).

Alile Sharon Larkin, a black filmmaker whose best known film is *A Different Image* (1982), states in her article "Black Women

Filmmakers Defining Ourselves: Feminism in Our Own Voice" that "feminism succumbs to racism when it segregates black women from black men and dismisses our history. The assumption that black women and white women share identical or similar histories and experiences presents an important problem...Feminism must address these issues, otherwise its ahistorical approach towards black women can and does maintain institutional racism" (158-159). This speaks to the struggle women are having in that it is not just male to female but also non-black to black.

Another filmmaker who also provokes but perhaps not to the same extent *Warrior Masks* provokes is Mira Nair of India who deals with cultural and ethnic complexities in such films as *Mississippi Masala* (1991), *Salaam Bombay!* (1988), *India Cabaret* (1986). Of note is Nair's comment with regard to her interaction with Hollywood executives who wanted to "whiten" her films (Foster 119). Not pleased with just dealing with her own people, Nair took on the project about immigrant exiles from Cuba which became *The Perez Family* (1995).

Perhaps women in the Middle East and Africa have had perhaps more difficulty breaking barriers; however, Hamid Naficy of Iran states that women since the 1990s have been able to enter various areas in film (Naficy in Kindem 112), others still report difficulties. As Manthia Diawara of Senegal explains women directors are often overlooked if not ignored even at film conferences such that Mali filmmaker Kadiatou Konate criticized the attendees at a recent film conference for wanting women to follow traditional roles and who instead believes that women need to define their own destinies and break with traditions (Diawara in Kindem 132-133).

Closer to the USA, we have Mexican cinema which began in 1897 and which unfortunately has lost its silent era films; however, of note is Mimí Derba, a popular stage actress, who along with Enrique Rosas co founded Azteca Films, producing its first film *En defensa propria* (*In Self Defense*) in 1917 (Mora 20). Maria Novaro of Mexico is perhaps best known for her film *Danzón* (1992). She frankly states "I like it very much when people come away thinking 'only a woman could have made that film'" (Golden 24). In a very macho world, a female dancer is valued less when she loses her male dance partner, even if she is one of the best. As

Gabriel García Márquez explains, Novaro "is trying to reveal something about the condition of women in Mexico" (Golden 24). However, the Mexican condition, one of white vs. Indian and class, is a complicated one and one that predates Hernán Cortés's encounter with the Aztecs and more importantly La Malinche. As Ana M. López states: "The melodramatic is deeply embedded in Mexican and Hispanic culture and intersects with the three master narratives of Mexican society: religion, nationalism, and modernization" (507). The Spanish cultural history of especially the Southwest, beginning with its disassembly with Mexico's independence in 1810 and later Texas' independence in 1836 and the loss of most of Mexico's territory in 1848 from Texas to California, is again coming into play as Mexicans make up the majority of Latinos, now the largest minority, in the USA. Certainly recent films such as *Frida* (2002), about Mexican artist Frida Kahlo—no doubt influenced by Mexican director Paul Leduc's original *Frida* (1986)—directed by Julie Taymor and *Spanglish* (2004) directed by James L. Brooks, which deals with current cross-cultural issues between Anglos and Mexicans, among others will continue to make their way to cinema screens.

The other part of the Mexican struggle is rooted in the Catholic faith, a male dominated hierarchy, which brought down the America's first feminist Sor Juana Inés de la Cruz, a Mexican nun born in 1651 in Spanish Mexico, and the Virgin Guadalupe, a Native Mexican apparition of the Blessed Virgin Mary. Tied to this tradition is La Malinche or Malintzin Tenepal, commonly known as *la Chingada* (*the fucked one*). La Malinche was the Aztec princess who submitted to Hernán Cortés, becoming his courtesan and who handed her people over to the conquistadores (López 508). However, Chicana writers and scholars including Cherríe Moraga have reinterpreted La Malinche as the savior of her people, for the Aztecs would have perished under unintentional Spanish biological warfare (small pox, influenza, etc.) and gunpowder; instead by marrying the 'devilish enemy' *la raza* (the people) of La Malinche have survived to this day, though transformed by language, culture, and ethnic interracial marriages. Nonetheless, skin color still impinges on class dynamics (Pettit). The Mexican films mentioned by both male and female directors reflect similar struggles women have had in the USA, though the Mexican struggle has been a more complicated one, given that USA Mexicans found their social standing diminished in what was once Mexican territory, i.e., the Greater Southwest.

Argentine feminist filmmaker María Luisa Bemberg brought the life of Sor Juana Inés de la Cruz, the nun, to film in her masterpiece *Yo, la peor de todas* (*I, The Worst of All*) (1989). With an international cast in an Argentine-French-Spanish co-production which was based on the biography of Inés de la Cruz by Mexican poet Octavio Paz. The film portrays the difficulties Inés de la Cruz encountered with ecclesiastical authorities who persecuted her willingness to speak up about the abuse of women, both white and non-white, at the time. "While seemingly a break in period and subject matter, *Yo, la peor de todas* reveals Bemberg's strong authorial signature in its focus on the efforts to force the submission of women to patriarchal institutions, here represented by the Spanish Church officials of colonial Mexico" (Wexman 124). Of late, women clergy in the USA have experienced a unified attack on their religious advancements within certain Christian denominations; however, a major film about this phenomenon has not come to light as of yet.

Unfortunately, the plight of Natives in Mexico as well as in the USA and Canada continues, such that Canadian Native American filmmaker Alanis Obomsawin has focused on the need to document the cultural traditions and lives of Native American peoples in such films as *Mother of Many Children* (1977) and *Poundmaker's Lodge: A Healing Place* (1987), which deals with the tragedies alcohol has created for Native Americans (Foster 146-147). With the recent opening of the Museum of the American Indian at the Smithsonian Institution, hopefully there will be more films that deal with the struggle that women continue to experience within their own communities and across communities because of gender, skin color, or class.

## Conclusion

The historical thread of women in film is quite immense but one can say that the images of women projected are in fact a reflection of life as seen by others within a given timeframe as well as a reflection of life as one would like for life to be. As writers, directors, and actors attempt to leave their legacy in the form of film, I believe Kaplan aptly states the course that is needed: "What rather has to happen is that we move beyond long-held cultural and linguistic patterns of oppositions: male/female (as these terms currently signify); dominant/submissive; active/passive; nature/ civilization; order/ chaos; matriarchal/ patriarchal. If rigidly defined sex differences have been constructed around fear of the other, we need to think about ways of transcending a polarity that has only brought us all pain" (135).

It is important to note that what many of the female directors have in common is a desire to portray the difficulties people encounter thereby their films become a social and political means to bring these issues to the attention of the majority who do not have to endure such hardships, discrimination, racism, sexism, and such atrocities done to humanity in the name of advancement of one's culture, political agenda, or greed.

# Works Cited

Braun, Eric. *Frightening the Horses: Gay Icons of the Cinema.* London: Reynolds & Hearn Ltd, 2002.

Bryant, Wayne M. *Bisexual Characters in Film: From Anaïs to Zee.* New York: Harrington Park Press, 1997.

Crisp, Colin. *The Classic French Cinema: 1930-1960.* Bloomington: Indiana University Press, 1997.

Darren, Alison. *Lesbian Film Guide.* New York: Cassell, 2000.

Diawara, Manthia. "Senegal," in *The International Movie Industry*, ed. Gorham Kindem. Carbondale: Southern Illinois University Press, 2000.

Foster, Gwendolyn Audrey. *Women Filmmakers of the African & Asian Diaspora: Decolonizing the Gaze, Locating Subjectivity.* Carbondale: Southern Illinois University Press, 1997.

Giron, Robert L. "Gender and African Diaspora Issues in Film." *Community College Humanities Review*, (19, Fall 1998).

Haskell, Molly. *From Reverence to Rape.* New York: Penguin, 1973.

Larkin, Alile Sharon. "Black Women Film-Makers Defining Ourselves: Feminism in Our Own Voices." *Female Spectators.* Ed. E. Deidre Pribram. London: Verso, 1988.

López, Ana M. "Tears and Desire: Women and Melodrama," in *Feminism & Film*, ed. E. Ann Kaplan. Oxford: Oxford University Press, 2000.

Kaplan, E. Ann. "Introduction" and "Is the Gaze Male?" *Feminism & Film.* Oxford: Oxford University Press, 2000.

Klotman, Phyllis R. and Gloria J. Gibson. *Frame by Frame II: A Filmography of the African American Image, 1978-1994.* Bloomington: Indiana University Press, 1997.

Mayne, Judith. *The Woman at the Keyhole: Feminism and Women's Cinema.* Bloomington: Indiana University Press, 1990.

Mora, Carl J. *Mexican Cinema: Reflections of a Society 1896-1988*. Berkeley: University of California Press, 1982.

Moraga, Cherríe. "From a Long Line of Vendidas: Chicanas and Feminism," in *Feminist Studies/Critical Studies*, ed. Teresa de Lauretis. Bloomington: Indiana University Press, 1986.

Murray, Raymond. *Images in the Dark: An Encyclopedia of Gay and Lesbian Film and Video*. Philadelphia: TLA Publications, 1994.

Naficy, Hamid. "Iran," in *The International Movie Industry*, ed. Gorham Kindem. Carbondale: Southern Illinois University Press, 2000.

Mulvey, Laura. "Visual Pleasure and Narrative Cinema." *Screen*, 16:3 (Autumn, 1975).

Parmar, Pratibha. "That Moment of Emergence." *Queer Looks: Perspectives on Lesbian and Gay Film and Video*. Ed. Pratibha Parmar, John Greyson, and Martha Gever. New York: Routledge, 1993.

Pietropaolo, Laura and Ada Testaferri. *Feminisms in the Cinema*. Bloomington: Indiana University Press, 1995.

Pettit, Arthur G. *Images of the Mexican American in Fiction and Film*. College Station: Texas A&M University Press, 1980.

Weiss, Andrea. *Vampires & Violets: Lesbians in Film*. New York: Penguin Books, 1992.

Wexman, Virginia Wright. *Film and Authorship*. New Jersey: Rutgers University Press, 2003.

White, Patricia. "Feminism and Film," in *The Oxford Guide to Film Studies*, ed. John Hill and Pamela Church Gibson. Oxford: Oxford University Press, 1998.

# Their Eyes Were Watching God: Subversive Quest for A Woman's Voice
## by Brianne Friel

Zora Neale Hurston, African-American woman writer of the 1920s, managed to publish prolifically through the mostly-male, mostly-white publishing industry despite intense criticism from her male colleagues. She did this, as women have since the advent of print, by using keen rhetorical skill.[1] Hurston's most popular novel, *Their Eyes Were Watching God*, for example, uses a safe, conventional romance plot and seemingly conservative narrative choices to mask the subversive plot that lurks beneath the surface: the quest for an African American woman's right to speak, to tell her own story, and ultimately, to be the author of her own life.[2] Evidence within the text overwhelmingly reveals that the question of romance is raised only to be rejected, that a more subtle, more disruptive quest has undermined it and taken its place. It seems that the author sets up the conventional love quest not only as a decoy for her more revolutionary plot, but also as a foil to be toppled by the more satisfying way of life that Janie ultimately enjoys. Part of Janie's victory is learning to be her own person, and part of her victory is finding a voice that is right for her; the author's "conservative" narrative choices actually support these discoveries.

On one level, *Their Eyes Were Watching God* is a romance, a safe and predictable search for a woman's mate. Janie is motivated, in part, by a dream for sexual and romantic fulfillment, and the initial impetus for Janie's voyage is a man—Joe Starks—who takes her from another man. The matches that the plot produces for Janie become increasingly more appropriate, culminating in Janie's relationship with Tea Cake, described as an ideal lover. But where the romance quest should culminate—on Janie and Tea

Cake's wedding night—is left a void. Not only is her husband absent from their marriage bed, but he also has stolen Janie's money to gamble with new friends and impress new women. The climax of the novel takes place instead when Janie shoots and kills him. The author takes great pains to justify Janie's shooting of Tea Cake: he was bitten by a rabid dog; he was no longer himself; he threatened to kill himself and Janie. It was his loaded weapon that Janie fired, and she only took it from him when he pointed it at her. Yet Janie still shoots and kills the man who should represent her ultimate fulfillment.

Further undermining the romance is the subplot of Mrs. Tyler, a woman from Janie's community. Mrs. Tyler's love affairs demonstrate the ugly underside of sexual politics and provide a foil to Janie and Tea Cake's romance. Her story appears at key moments to warn and remind Janie and the audience of what happens to women who put their faith in their sexual attractiveness to men. Mrs. Tyler embodies male exploitation of female sexuality: old and wrinkled, trussed and corseted, dyed and powdered, hobbling around the streets in stiletto heels a size too small, Mrs. Tyler is taken advantage of by a string of younger men, robbed, and left to beg on the streets like a stray dog. Mrs. Tyler is introduced in the novel at key points: when Janie begins her relationship with Tea Cake, before Janie's wedding, and, most significantly, on Janie's wedding night. In fact, the specter of Mrs. Tyler replaces Tea Cake in Janie's marriage-bed when Tea Cake disappears, for the image of Mrs. Tyler "made itself into pictures and hung around Janie's bedside all night long" (272). Already, on her wedding night, Janie fears for where her relationship with Tea Cake might lead her.

The most radical anti-romance message in the novel, though, comes from Janie's grandmother, Nanny. Nanny introduces a heavy dose of reality to the love-struck Janie when she teaches her (and the audience) about social injustices that end in the mistreatment of black girls like Janie:

> de white man is de ruler of everything as fur as Ah been able tuh find out. Maybe it's some place way off in de ocean where de black man is in power, but we don't know nothin' but what we see. So de white man throw down de load and tell de nigger man tuh pick it up. He pick it up because he have to, but he don't tote it. He hand it to his womenfolks. De nigger woman is de mule uh de world so fur as Ah can see. (186)

Janie's relationships with men illustrate the power imbalance that Nanny describes here, making a love between equals impossible. In Nanny's experience, love is nothing but a trap to keep women "pullin' and uh haulin' and sweatin' and doin' from can't see in de mornin' till can't see at night" (193), and sex is essentially exploitative, since she can't die easy thinking "de menfolks white or black is makin' a spit cup outa you" (190).

Nanny tries to open Janie's eyes with the facts of her own history, which adds another layer of grim realism to the novel. Nanny describes how, when she was held in slavery, she was raped by a slaveholder. Not yet healed from the birth of his child, she is forced to flee from his sadistic wife who promises to sell Nanny's child, beat Nanny to death, and "stand de loss" (189) of her. Nanny's child is, in turn, raped by her schoolteacher. Nanny herself refuses to choose marriage as a refuge because "Ah didn't want nobody mistreating mah baby" (190).

Nanny views men as essentially predatory, so much so that she takes for granted that any man she brings into her home would abuse her daughter. This representation of men as predators recurs in the depiction of men in droves who attack Mrs. Tyler like wolves and leave her in tatters on the street, and again in those who appear out of nowhere to "protect" Janie after she is left a rich widow. It is reinforced by the Eatonville men who agree they would kill a woman "cemetery dead" (235) for embarrassing her husband and by the community of men on the muck who envy Tea Cake's right "tuh whip uh tender woman lak Janie" (294). Janie's relationships with men further bear out Nanny's fears of violence. Janie is kept down and forced within herself during her marriage to Joe, as described by a violent metaphor: "She was a rut in the road. Plenty of life beneath the surface but it was kept beaten down by the wheels" (236). Joe views Janie as a possession. He expects obedience and silence, and he beats her when he is dissatisfied. When he doesn't like his dinner, Joe "slapped Janie until she had a ringing sound in her ears..." (232). Tea Cake is no better, for he beats her in a possessive rage, and "being able to whip her reassured him in possession" (294).

Nanny is quite possibility the most feminist character in the novel, not only warning Janie about the traps of romantic love, but also replacing Janie's ambition to find a man with a quest for a public voice. Since Nanny's society would not allow her to speak, she entrusts Janie with the difficult responsibility of finding a way to speak, not only for herself, but also for the generations of women who went before her. As Nanny explains:

> Ah wanted to preach a great sermon about colored women sittin' on high, but they wasn't no pulpit for me.... So whilst Ah was tendin' you of nights Ah said Ah'd save de text for you. (187)

Nanny had a message she felt called to share, but there was no place where she could express herself, and no audience who would hear it. So she decides to teach Janie the message that women can accomplish great things. But "the text" is not only the message of a sermon, but also words themselves, for Janie must be a master of words to find a way to deliver this sermon. This feminist message is sacred, as expressed through the religious imagery, not only in its topic, but also in the very fact of its delivery, since it will speak for generations of women now gone. And the novel enumerates Janie's qualifications for the task: she is a gifted rhetorician with a sacred calling to speak, a "born orator" who can "put jus' de right words" to the community's thoughts, the mark of a true poet.

Janie's first step towards gaining a voice is realizing that she has private, internal thoughts, beliefs, and ideas that her husband Joe and the rest of the world cannot control.[3] As she becomes more aware of what is important to her, she suffers "many silent rebellions" (218) over injustices done to Mrs. Robbins, a pathetically needy woman, and a defenseless yellow mule, both low in the social hierarchy and abused. When the men torture the mule, Janie remains silent, but "a little war of defense for helpless things was going on inside her." Yet her silence is misleading, for, now, "the stillness was the sleep of swords" (240). Immediately after her revelation that she "had an inside and an outside now and suddenly she knew how not to mix them" (233), she does "what she had never done before, that is, thrust herself into the conversation." She speaks up about the men's abuse of Mrs. Robbins and informs them that women, too, have an inner life, an intellect and a spirit: "sometimes God gits familiar wid us womenfolks too and talks His inside business" (235).[4] Not only does Janie learn to speak up to Joe, but the words she uses against him are powerful. Scholar Henry Louis Gates describes the scene in which Janie speaks up to Joe as "truly the first feminist critique of the fiction of authority of the male voice, and its sexism, in the Afro-American tradition" (207). Janie's community view her words as a criticism that destroys Joe.

When Janie comes home alone, thoroughly in charge now of her own life and beholden to no one, she successfully ends her journey. The true climax of the novel occurs when Janie meets *herself* on her "honeymoon" as a single woman. Janie's solo homecoming after Tea Cake's death has all the fulfillment of a true honeymoon. The advancing evening of her first night at home alone makes Janie "think about that room upstairs—her bedroom" (332-3). The narrator describes with loving lyricism Janie's newfound self-actualization as she climbs the stairs to bed by herself: "the light in her hand was like a spark of sun-stuff washing her face in fire" (333). When Janie gets to her bedroom, it offers the promise and hope lacking in her marriage bed. In fact, the spirit of Janie's marriage to Joe had "left the bedroom," replaced by a "spirit like a Virgin Mary image in church" (232)—celibacy enshrined, hardly a fit image for a marriage bed. But the death of her husbands breathes fresh life into her bedroom: "Now, in her room, the place tasted fresh again. The wind through the open windows had broomed out all the fetid feeling of absence and nothingness" (333). Her "journey to the horizons," not for one true love but "in search of *people*," is fulfilled on this night as she pulls in "her horizon like a great fish-net. Pulled it from around the waist of the world and draped it over her shoulder. So much of life in its meshes!" (333). Her horizon, which she once believed was "tight enough to choke her" (247) is now as expansive as the circumference of the globe; alone, she is free to face all of life unfettered. When Janie thinks about people like herself who are made out of "stuff that sung all the time and glittered all over" but are covered with mud (247), she is thinking about the songs that dwell within us all that need to released, about the stories waiting to be told and the obstacles in their way.

When Janie tells her story to her friend Pheoby, she fulfills the purpose her grandmother set for her of learning to speak and finding a forum for her speech. Janie will tell the tale that speaks in many ways for women of every generation. Yet Hurston depicts

Janie speaking privately to Pheoby, who will then transmit Janie's story to the community, instead of showing Janie speak directly to the community. Similarly, Hurston chooses not to show Janie speaking directly to the jury as she fights for her life in a court of law; instead, we hear about her speech second-hand.

If Janie now has gained a voice, why doesn't she address the community herself—why doesn't she give a speech as men in the community stand around and listen? For one thing, that would not have been realistic. Janie needs to find a way—and she does—of transferring her message in spite of her gender, which excludes her from public speech. To show Janie addressing the community in a public setting might also have been too much for Hurston's audiences—*when the content and context of the novel are as radical as they are.* Male critics of the Harlem Renaissance already had proven unsympathetic to much of Hurston's work, and Hurston had to imagine a white publishing industry and readership as well.[5] For Hurston to embed Janie's voice, as she does, protects Janie as it protects the novel itself from seeming too radical and thereby risking destruction. And, through rhetorical strategy, Janie's voice is preserved, for, although Janie declines to give her speech to the community, the *readers* of the novel hear Janie tell her story to Pheoby. Also, Janie is really co-narrator, with Pheoby, of her story, since, as Janie puts it, "mah tongue is in mah friend's mouf" (179); Pheoby becomes a mediator, as a less-rebellious woman, between Janie and the community. We continue to hear Janie's voice, throughout the novel, through the narrator's free-indirect discourse: that is, the narrator, who is sympathetic to Janie, often slips into a voice that sounds a lot like Janie's. Hurston the rhetorician functions both as Janie, the individual seeking to tell her story, and as Pheoby, the mediator who will carry it to an audience that cannot be relied upon to be sympathetic, so she walks a line between making her point and making compromises. In similar fashion, the second-hand depiction of Janie's speech in the courtroom is again something of a narrative trick, since it masks for the audience the fact that Janie has shot and killed a man, and now stands up to a mixed-race, mixed-gender courtroom to defend herself, wins her case, and is freed.

In spite of the narrative choices which don't allow Janie's speech to be heard by large groups at important moments, Janie successfully finds a voice that is right for her. That voice is not the dominating voice of white society with which Joe is clearly aligned and which Tea Cake clearly admires.[6] Hurston uses the same strategies to present Janie's voice that she learned from a lifetime of studying and documenting the African-American vernacular, the oral tradition that kept history and stories alive for generations to come, the strategies that grew out of power imbalances and a love of telling stories. There is much to admire in this voice, born of the oral tradition and a need to be wary. When Janie speaks to Pheoby, who in turn transmits the story to the rest of the community, she follows the oral tradition which her grandmother patterned for her and which Hurston admires and seeks to emulate within the confines of the printed word. While Hurston can't actually tell the story to only one individual and publish it at the same time, she can dramatize the intimate scenario of a *dialogue in which the person listening is just as important as the one speaking*, where one person does not need to be silenced or dominated for the other to speak. Under this model, it is perfectly natural that Janie's story will be transmitted by mouth through numerous small groups. In fact, by admitting her story into the oral tradition that is beloved by the community, its prosperity is guaranteed. Janie and Pheoby constitute a community sharing important stories, a community of women who now join the ranks of the "porch-talkers" from which they previously have been excluded. Not only will Janie's stories be passed along to the community, but also, because the story is published as well, to Hurston's contemporary and future generations of readers. When we overhear Janie telling her story to Pheoby, or when we hear second-hand about Janie's audacious self-defense in court, we have the illusion that we, the readers, join in the oral tradition as listeners as well.

Not only does Hurston choose not to use a voice of traditional power for Janie, but also, the novel criticizes that voice, and, ultimately, Janie rejects it. Joe, for example, is depicted making plenty of speeches, yet his voice ultimately is less successful than Janie's, for it dies with him. Joe has a "big voice" that monopolizes speech and dominates others. Not only does he require silence from his wife, but he also needs to overtake her mind until it "had tuh be squeezed and crowded out tuh make room for yours in me" (224). Joe demands the silence of all those less powerful than himself, and he carefully cultivates and enforces Janie's silence, speaking for her and refusing to let her speak to their neighbors when they arrive in town. He literally shuts her inside the store they operate and inside herself, keeping her away from the commerce of language and life, for "when Lige or Sam or Walter or some of the other big picture talkers were using a side of the world for a canvas, Joe would hustle her off inside the store" (217). He chastises her for "getting' too moufy" (235) and, on his deathbed, leaves her with this epitaph: "Shut up!" (244).

Joe takes his need to be heard to such extremes that he forgets to listen to others. He doesn't take place in any dialogue; he lectures. And he doesn't allow Janie any room to speak for herself, to think for herself, or to be her own person. Not only does this stifle Janie, but it hurts Joe as well. In fact, Joe can never learn or grow because he never listens to another person's voice. Really hearing another person's perspective is frightening because it means being open to changing your own mind or even the way that you live. Listening leads to accepting others' humanity, and so to equality. Suppressing others' right to speak is a form of brutality that Janie links to other forms of oppression: "Have yo' way all yo' life, trample and mash down and then die ruther than tuh let yo'self heah 'bout it." What she says to Joe, who is associated with white values, stands as an indictment of white American society: "you was so busy worshippin' de works of yo' own hands, and cuffin' folks around in their minds till you didn't see uh whole heap uh things you could have" (244). In fact, Janie believes Joe has traded in his humanity for a dominating voice, has made "a voice out of a man" (245).[7] Joe's inability to listen to others not only kills him spiritually and emotionally, but literally, as well, for he refuses to heed Janie's pleas to seek the advice of a doctor, and so he dies of kidney failure.

Tea Cake too shuts out other voices with his, a fatal flaw for him as well as Joe. Tea Cake won't follow Native Americans fleeing a hurricane because "Indians don't know much uh nothin'.... Else dey'd own dis country still" (301-2). He only wants to hear the most powerful voices: since "de white folks ain't gone nowhere. Dey oughta know if it's dangerous" (301-2), he won't go, either. Trapped in the hurricane, he continues to shut out the voices around him. Ignoring his friend's entreaties to seek higher ground, he is swept away by the floods and bitten by a frantic, rabid dog also trapped in the hurricane. Even then, he refuses Janie's offers to get help for his dog bite, and perishes as a result of the madness that ensues.

Unlike Joe and Tea Cake, Janie is skilled at reading nature, communing with God, and understanding mysterious silences, all important facets of communication. She listens to the languages of many things and communes with nature, understanding "the words of the trees and the wind" and speaking "to falling seeds..." (194). Those who successfully escape the hurricane are skilled at paying attention to others, even those seemingly lesser than they (the Native Americans fleeing the area), and the hidden signs of nature (the crows flying North). Those people like Tea Cake who looked to the "big" voices of power found that, at the moment of crisis, there was no big voice to help them out. As they huddle in their home against the deadly storm, the narrator informs us, "The time was past for asking the white folks what to look for through that door. Six eyes were questioning *God*" (304). Each person now must be able to listen to God; the structure that has monopolized speech, silenced others, and given the impression of power is not to be trusted. More important now than bullying others by having the last word is the ability to listen, specifically to read silences and see hidden meanings: "They seemed to be staring at the dark, but their eyes were watching God" (305), a message so important that it is underlined by the title of the book.

Janie's success is in understanding those who are less powerful than she, even in reading silences, since she must speak for past generations for whom there is no written record. Her journey is as much about understanding as it is communicating, and when she communicates, it is in a gentle, non-dominating way, a way that respects the other person (the listener) and much as it values its own voice. Instead of emulating Joe or Tea Cake, and without taking on the dominant social structure's overpowering speech strategies, Janie instead has modeled another rhetorical strategy, one that relies on conversation, on listening, understanding, and reading silences, rather than on force. Yes, Janie has been excluded from power in her community, as has Hurston, but both borrow from what Eric J. Sundquist calls "the art of the African-American vernacular" the features of "indirection, and silence" (66) to create a feminist model of communication that works both for Janie and for Hurston's novel.

In spite of the limitations imposed on Janie's, and, indeed, on Hurston's voices because of their gender, we must remember that as long as there is conversation, as long as multiple voices are allowed, there is hope for response and of improvement, both within and without one's own community. Although Janie does not tell her story directly to her own community, her story will survive, and it will be passed along: we learn this much about the oral tradition from the novel itself. This, indeed, is the beauty of the oral folk tradition that Hurston devoted her life to chronicling; this is the hope for the salvation of the women of the community and the hope for reconciliation among men and women. Because she is able to put her words in the mouth of a friend, a person who can speak from and to several communities and audiences at the same time, Janie is able to tell her tale, and because Hurston is capable of inventing narrative strategies that made her works more acceptable to a general audience, her literature has survived to enjoy great popularity and acclaim today. Janie's silences—and Hurston's omissions—do demonstrate, as Mary Helen Washington points out, "women's exclusion from power, particularly from the power of...speech" (98). On the other hand, we must remember that, whatever gender limitations Janie suffers, Hurston herself had to contend with as a female author writing about a rebellious female hero who ends the novel loving herself. Any narrative choices, or compromises, within the novel must be seen within this context.

## Works Cited

Bakhtin, M.M. *The Dialogic Imagination*. Ed. Michael Holquist, trans. Caryl Emerson and Michael Holquist. Austin: U. Texas P, 1981.

Callahan, Joh. "'Mah Tongue is in Mah Friend's Mouf'." *In The African American Grain: The Pursuit of Voice in Twentieth-Century Black Fiction*. Urbana: U of Illinois P, 1988. 115-49.

Carby, Hazel V. "The Politics of Fiction, Anthropology, and the Folk: Zora Neale Hurston." *New Essays on* Their Eyes Were Watching God. Ed. Michael Awkward. Cambridge: Cambridge UP, 1990: 71-93.

DuPlessis, Rachel Blau. "Power, Judgment, and Narrative in a Work of Zora Neale Hurston: Feminist Cultural Studies." *New Essays on* Their Eyes Were Watching God, ed. Michael Awkward. Cambridge: Cambridge UP, 1990: 95-123.

Gates, Henry Louis Jr. *The Signifying Monkey: A Theory of African-American Literary Criticism*. New York: Oxford UP, 1988.

Hemenway, Robert. Zora Neale Hurston: A Literary Biography. Urbana: U of Illinois P, 1977.

Hurston, Zora Neale. *Dust Tracks on a Road. Hurston: Folklore, Memoirs, & Other Writings*. Ed. Cheryl Wall. New York: Library of America, 1995: 559-808.

———. *Mules and Men. Hurston: Folklore, Memoirs, & Other Writings*. Ed. Cheryl Wall. New York: Library of America, 1995: 9-267.

———. *Their Eyes Were Watching God. Hurston: Novels and Stories*. Ed. Cheryl Wall. New York: Library of America, 1995: 175-333.

Johnson, Barbara. "Metaphor, Metonymy, and Voice in Zora Neale Hurston's *Their Eyes Were Watching God*." *Black Literature and Literary Theory*. Ed. Henry-Louis Gates. New York: Methuen P, 1984: 204-19.

Lanser, Susan Sniader. *Fictions of Authority: Women Writers and Narrative Voice*. Ithaca: Cornell UP, 1992.

Sundquist, Eric J. "The Drum with the Man Skin": *Jonah's Gourd Vine*. 39-66 in *Zora Neale Hurston: Critical Perspectives Past and Present*. Ed. Henry Louis Gates, Jr. and K.A. Appiah. New York: Amistad P, 1993.

Washington, Mary Helen. "'I Love the Way Janie Crawford Left Her Husbands'" Emergent Female Hero." 98-109 in *Zora Neale Hurston: Critical Perspectives Past and Present*. Ed. Henry Louis Gates, Jr. and K.A. Appiah. New York: Amistad P, 1993.

## Notes

1. Although writing, especially for public consumption, has not historically been considered a woman's work, resourceful women long have found ways to get their ideas and words into print. Some of these strategies were to publish anonymously, use pseudonyms, make excuses or "apologies" for their work, and confine themselves to the acceptable, "feminine" topics of religion or domesticity, or to genres that gave the illusion of privacy, such as letter-writing or diaries. To give just one famous example for each category: Jane Austen published anonymously; Charlotte Bronte and her sisters used male pseudonyms; Margery Kempe's religious visions were transcribed for her; Anne Bradstreet justified or "apologized" for her writing in the preface to her volume of poems, and Lady Mary Wortley Montagu circulated her writing in letters to her friends.

2. Mary Helen Washington discusses the text's oscillation between a romance and a quest plot, between presenting Janie as a hero or a heroine. Washington cites Rachel Blau Du Plessis' definition of a hero as "a central character whose activities, growth, and insight are given much narrative attention and authorial interest," while a heroine remains "the object of male attention or rescue" (qtd. in Washington, n.19, p. 109).

3. She "sat and watched the shadow of herself going about tending store and prostrating itself before Jody, while all the time she herself sat under a shady tree with the wind blowing through her hair and her clothes" (236). Janie's silent resistance of Joe, giving him only "what she didn't value" (236) and keeping the rest to herself, is reminiscent of the "featherbed resistance" that Hurston describes as characteristically African-American in *Mules and Men*: "I'll set something outside the door of my mind for him to play with and handle. He can read my writing but he sho' can't read my mind. I'll put this play toy in his hand, and he will seize it and go away. Then I'll say my say and sing my song" (10).

4   This ability to separate her inside and her outside leads to an acquisition of voice because, as Barbara Johnson perceives, the separation of internal and external meanings is prerequisite to figurative language. Johnson correlates Janie's awareness of a dual existence to her ability to speak: "Janie's acquisition of the power of voice thus grows not out of her identity but out of her division into inside and outside. Knowing how not to mix them is knowing that articulate language requires the co-presence of two distinct poles, not their collapse into oneness." Johnson explains that, just as understanding the difference between internal and external identity leads to voice, reduction of identity "has as its necessary consequence aphasia, silence, the loss of the ability to speak." So the rhetoric Janie gains "grows out of her ability not to mix inside with outside, not to pretend that there is no difference, but to assume and articulate the incompatible forces involved in her own division. The sign of an authentic voice is thus not self-identity but self-difference" (212).

5   In *Fictions of Authority: Women Writers and Narrative Voice*, Susan Sniader Lanser observes that female authors often compensate for powerful female protagonists and/or unconventional plot lines with narrative compromises: the more radical the story of the protagonist, the more conservative the narrative form. One way that women writers could make up for the fact that they themselves were engaging in public discourse was by placing their female protagonists in private spaces. Hurston's framing device, as well as the use of free indirect discourse, negotiate with literary conventions while approximating the protagonist's voice so that "the narrative form Hurston adopts allows her to have it both ways, creating a private structure in which one black woman is alleged to tell her story to another, but using a heterodiegetic voice to authorize Janie's story for a public readership presumed to be racially and sexually mixed" (205). Lanser also suggests that the courtroom audience, which consists of white men and women and black men but apparently no black women, "parallels the complex and divided readership that Hurston herself faced writing a feminist novel in a male-

dominated Harlem Renaissance within a white literary establishment" (205).

6   Joe Starks represents the worst of white materialism and exploitation, both northern and southern: he is "kind of portly like rich white folks" (201); he bosses his neighbors until they "murmured hotly about slavery being over" (211); he owns a spittoon "just like his used-to-be-bossman used to have in his bank up there in Atlanta"; and his home makes the rest of the town look "like servant's quarters surrounding the 'big house'" (212). Tea cake won't evacuate the flood site in a hurricane because "de white folks ain't gone nowhere. Dey oughta know if it's dangerous" (301-2).

7   Janie, on the other hand, gains in self-awareness as the novel progresses, as marked by mirror metaphors. Nanny's wish is that Janie be able "to look upon yo'self" (190), but at first she cannot pick herself out of a photograph: "So Ah ast, 'where is me? Ah don't see me'" (191). Janie's first look at herself from the outside occasions a racial awareness that ripens as the novel progresses. As Henry Louis Gates points out, Janie "passes" in reverse; as she does so, she gains racial awareness and pride, moving south, marrying a darker man, and learning racial pride. She is called "Alphabet" as a child "'cause so many people had done named me different names" (181-2). After Janie is liberated from her silencing marriage to Joe, she remembers a pact she made with herself: "Years ago, she had told her girl self to wait for her in the looking glass.... She went over to the dresser and looked hard at her skin and features" (245). Janie has fulfilled her childhood wish to be able to look on—and recognize—herself.

# Giving Voice to the Unspeakable: Contemporary Poems by Women

by Kay Bosgraaf

At no other time than the present has literature offered so great a chorus of women's voices, freeing their poems from the expectations of mainstream poetry created and perpetuated by men. Contemporary women poets are revising what is seen and heard in poetry, making the invisible visible, the hidden revealed, and the silenced heard. For many contemporary women poets, poetry is a vehicle for living in and experiencing the moment fully; for many traditional poets, the point of view of the poet has been that of the observer, not the actor. This new perspective views poetry as a process more than a product, as a way to enter life rather than to order, understand, and record it. As these writers create their own rules for writing poetry, they free themselves to write about new subjects such as female forebears, mother-child relationships, child sexual abuse, and clinical depression, amongst others. In so doing, they actively question what has been left in the margins or outside the scope of poetry. Contemporary women poets also provide a fresh perspective on traditional themes such as death and dying. Finally, these writers celebrate traditional women's work by making it the subject of their poems and by borrowing its language for metaphors and images, no matter what the subject of the poems.

Whereas traditionally poetry has been a way of understanding, recording, and ordering existence, some contemporary women poets value writing a poem as a way of experiencing each moment in the fullest way. Jorie Graham discusses her own writing from the point of view of a participant. She says, "Through Poems, I've struggled to make sure I'm in life, as opposed to merely understanding it" and "Poetry has always seemed to me not so much a record of a life lived [than] as a way—through the act of composition—of experiencing an event I missed [by] just living it" (Cahill 16). Graham views the poem not as a final product but a means to more fully experience her own life; the writing of the poem transforms her own life. In contrast, Robert Frost says that writing poetry is his way of taking life by the throat, a way of ordering and acting upon life. Poets who are willing to be inside of each moment must be willing to suspend traditional definitions of intellect and meaning. Graham says that "Thinking deeply is feeling deeply. They're interchangeable" (Cahill 17). Such a view of the intellect implies that to gain knowledge and understanding, people must be aware of the emotions centered in their bodies and minds as they experience each moment, be willing to feel deeply, and participate in life rather than merely observe it.

Susan Mitchell's poem "Bird: A Memoir" echoes Graham's ideas about experiencing life without the traditional restraints of the intellect and the need for meaning. In one stanza of this long poem, she says,

> To disperse, to unfocus
> into showers of gold and tinsel is my one desire.
> Why must everything be dragged through intellect?
> I am sick of meaning. Today I shall throw myself away
> in puff after puff of furbish and spangle. (150-54)

Later in this poem Mitchell writes,

> To attend. To hear in *attention* the tension—and a tone
> tentative at first, but with listening, tonic. To be stretched
> on tenterhooks of aural surge. Not to miss out on anything:
> to make that my lifework. The ear excited for longer
> and longer until listening, breathless, cries out.
> Or, on a dare, slipping in and out of meaning, and in the wild
> screams of loss, filled full. Is that fulfillment? (267-273)

What Graham says about the process of writing poetry, Mitchell says of living life itself: suspend life as it has been defined and be ready for all its realities and mysteries. No one can understand life without experiencing it, without feeling it.

This call to live life in its moments encourages women to write about new subjects as participants, not as observers. The personal experience of women, formerly considered too personal, private, unimportant, or shameful for poetry, has now very often become its subject and theme. Even though personal experience carries great authority, within the confines of traditional poetry personal experience is viewed as self-centered and superfluous, frivolous and even impolite. Graham says that "Thinking deeply is feeling deeply. They're interchangeable" (Cahill 17).

Two new and related subjects that contemporary women writers enjoy are their connection to their female past through mothers, grandmothers, and others, and their thoughts and feelings about motherhood. Eleanor Wilner believes "that it is the huge reservoir of unspoken inner life of the female past that drives and energizes the extraordinary tide of contemporary poetry by women" (xxv). Ample evidence can be cited to support Wilner's statement: Sonia Sanchez in "A Love Song for Spelman"; Florence Ladd in "Daughter of the Outer Banks" and "Ode to My Great Grandmother"; Cheryl Savageau in "Like a Good Joke: Grandma at Ninety"; Judith Ortiz Cofer in "Photographs of My Father" and "Cold as Heaven," and Jane Cooper in "My Mother in Three Acts." These are only a few examples of the numerous poets reaching back to connect with those females who came before them. Their efforts to connect with a female past are balanced by portrayals of specifically female roles in the present, particularly mothering, experienced by the poets and their speakers. Mary Jo Salter in "Liam," Ruth Stone in "The Ways of Daughters" and "The Trinity," and Carolyn Kizer in "Parents' Pantoum" are three of the many poets writing on the subject of mothering. Rita Dove devotes the entire volume *Mother Love* to the story of Demeter and Persephone, and Kate Daniels allocates thirty pages to mothering in "Portrait of the Artist as Mother" in *Four Testimonies*. Such celebration of women's past and present lives has not been so directly and abundantly presented before in poetry.

An excellent example of a poem that deals explicitly with unveiling the hidden is Maxine Kumin's "Photograph, Maryland Agricultural College Livestock Show, 1924." The speaker's desire to see past closed doors and beyond facades is the subject of her poem. Initially Kumin describes the men and their animals shown in the photograph: "Blond, wholesome, serene, / their white shirtsleeves rolled" are "these boys in white ducks" (1-3) with their sleek hogs and pedigreed calves. In the second and last stanza, she writes about what she believes is the larger, more complete picture:

> Mostly I think about
> the unseen mud and manure, flies
> and screwworms that connect these boys
> and their wildest hopes
> poised radiant between two wars
> while just out of reach of the lens
> in their stained bib overalls
> stand the farm laborers
>
> greasy with sweat
> and undoubtedly black. (9-18)

Kumin's observation of what is missing in a photograph becomes a strong statement against racial discrimination, exposed only when hidden subjects take their place in mainstream poetry.

Lucille Clifton, Sharon Olds, and Linda McCarriston are only a few of the strong voices in contemporary poetry that use the subjects of child abuse, child sexual abuse, and spousal abuse to insinuate that what has been hidden will be exposed. Many of their poems are difficult to read because the subjects are often rough and disturbing, painful and depressing; however, in the end the poetry conveys a calm sense of seeing life clearly and well, of approaching life with fervor and hope. By flouting the rules that define worthy subject matter, they give their readers permission to speak and write about *secrets*. Abuse can be seen as a metaphor for loss and abandonment or a symbol of human depravity, and although the physical reality of abuse itself is given prominence in these poems, the controlling themes often are hope and forgiveness. These themes are not new in poetry but are noteworthy because they are presented through the vehicle of abuse, a previously silenced subject.

In several of her poems, Clifton introduces her readers to the forbidden topic of sexual abuse of a child by a parent. This topic comes from her speaker's personal experience of being raped by her father. Her poem "night vision" presents a young girl routinely sexually abused by her father. One might expect this poem to be about revenge, but it is not. The poem does indeed expose the father, but, more importantly, it reveals a vision of hope that the girl is able to glean from the depths of this trauma:

> the girl fits her body in
> to the space between the bed
> and the wall. she is a stalk,

> exhausted. she will do some
> thing with this. she will
> surround these bones with flesh.
> she will cultivate night vision.
> she will train her tongue
> to lie still in her mouth and listen.
> the girl slips into sleep.
> her dream is red and raging.
> she will remember
> to build something human with it.

Note the repetition of the phrase "she will" throughout the poem: not "she will try" but "she will." She is enraged by her father's inhumanity but is determined that she will be human.

Many of Sharon Olds's poems deal with the speaker's need to forgive her mother and her father for their abuse of her, a clear example of the child being the adult. She is voicing the fact that children abused by their parents do not have parents in any meaningful sense of the word, an important new subject in poetry. The poems present graphic details of abuse in the context of the speaker's greater need to understand, forgive, and find peace in herself. Her poem "What if God" asks where God was when her mother was abusing her (the speaker). The poem begins with the question, "And what if God had been watching when my mother / came into my bed?" The last ten lines of the poem show the mother's warped perception of the presence of God and the speaker's feeling of being abandoned by both her mother and God:

> she said that all we did was done in His sight so
> what was He doing as He saw her weep in my
> hair and slip my soul from between my
> ribs like a tiny hotel soap, did He
> wash His hands of me as I washed my
> hands of Him? Is there a God in the house?
> Is there a God in the house? Then reach down and
> take that woman off that child's body,
> take that woman by the nape of the neck like a young cat and
> lift her up and deliver her over to me. (20-29)

The rage towards the mother exhibited here is repeated in many poems, but the poems are never only about the rage. "What if God" raises important spiritual questions about the presence or absence of God and asks how a child continues to live when the assumptions about God and mother are taken away, when there is no basis for trust.

In "After 37 Years My Mother Apologizes for My Childhood," Olds faces the emptiness that exists once a person gives up an old and consuming anger. As in "What if God," Olds's speaker strains towards something more than the events themselves. When her mother begs for forgiveness, the speaker says, "I could not / see what I would do with the rest of my life" (11-12). The poem concludes with these lines:

> I could not see what my
> days would be with you sorry, with
> you wishing you had not done it, the
> sky falling around me, its shards
> glistening in my eyes, your old soft
> body fallen against me in horror I
> took you in my arms, I said *It's all right,
> don't cry, it's all right,* the air filled with
> flying glass I hardly knew what I
> said or who I would be now that I had forgiven you. (17-26)

In "Late Poem to My Father," Olds's speaker looks at a photograph of her father as a boy standing in front of a fireplace with his family. She recognizes that he was not loved as a child, that he may have become ill with alcoholism in an effort to fill the empty space where love should have been. She believes

> ...something was
> not given to you, or something was
> taken from you that you were born with, so that
> even at 30 and 40 you set the
> oily medicine to your lips
> every night, the poison to help you
> drop down unconscious. (12-18)

She identifies with this unloved boy and is able to forgive her father:

> ...And what they did to you
> you did not do to me. When I love you now,
> I like to think I am giving my love
> directly to that boy in the fiery room,
> as if it could reach him in time. (25-29)

And so Olds presents the child as caretaker of the father and, in many other poems, of the mother. Here the speaker shows that understanding and accepting her father as a human being are relevant to learning to live with her own abuse. Olds is also suggesting that when abuse happens, it will no longer be a family's secret.

She has made public the subject of abuse, so public that it can appear in poems. Sexual or any other kind of abuse will no longer be hidden. Linda McCarriston's poem "Billy" is also about the abuse of a child by a parent. Here the speaker confronts the ugly visage of human depravity when her father sets Billy in a wooden barrel and proceeds to beat him. McCarriston is suggesting that when this type of situation develops in a family, it will not be hidden but bravely set forth because of its importance. She makes the same suggestion in her poem "A Castle in Lynn," where the speaker describes the father sexually abusing her and imagines him, now in his old age, thinking like the warped creature he was when younger:

> *I got there before*
> *the boys did*, he knows, hearing
> back to her pleading, back to her
> sobbing, to his own voice-over
> like his body over hers: laughter
>
> mocking, the elemental voice
> of the cock, unhearted, in its own
> quarter. *A man is king in his own*
> *castle,* he can still say, having got
>
> what he wanted: in a lifetime
> of used ones, second-hand, one girl
> he could spill like a shot of whiskey,
> the whore only he could call *daughter*. (20-32)

Here again McCarriston will not be content to hide this subject but will make it public because it is an important subject in the lives of women and girls. She gives this father a face and takes him out of hiding.

In McCarriston's poem "To Judge Faolain, Dead Long Enough: A Summons," she shows another kind of abuse traditionally experienced by women when church and state leaders fail to take into account the reality of women's lives. In this poem, the mother's abuse by the father is compounded by a judge who will not grant the mother a separation from the father but rather admonishes her and sends her home: "for the sake / of the family, the wife / must take the husband back to her bed" (18-20).

As do Clifton and Olds, McCarriston sees that human beings have the potential to rise above the inhumanity of abuse. "Healing the Mare" is a beautiful poem about the speaker's love for her horse:

> So both a child
> and a mother, with my sponge and
> my bucket, I come to anoint, to
> anneal the still weeping, to croon
> to you *baby poor baby* for the sake
> of the song, to polish you up
> for the sake of the touch, to a shine.
> As I soothe you I surprise wounds
> of my own this long time unmothered.
> As you stand, scathed and scabbed,
> with your head up, I swab. As you
> press, I lean into my own loving
> touch, for which no wound
> is too ugly. (19-32)

McCarriston presents a powerful image of the speaker facing ugly events of the past, moving beyond them, and, in this instance, healing self by reaching out to tend the wounds of another.

Clinical depression, formerly either hidden or tangential in poetry, has become more explicit in recent poetry by women. Sylvia Plath and Anne Sexton, like many other poets, described this severe mental anguish without actually naming it. In contrast, poet Jane Kenyon foregrounds it by naming it and its medical treatments. Her speakers describe how it feels to experience the coming of depression, of waiting to be taken to the hospital, of feeling an effective medication take hold, of going home. Her volume of poetry entitled *Constance* is interwoven with poems about clinical depression, leading the reader to experience and understand the speaker's fierce fight to dispel it. In Kenyon's poems mental illness comes out of the closet. She is declaring that this illness will no longer be removed to the third floor and hidden, but that it is a legitimate subject of poetry.

In the poem "Having it Out with Melancholy," Kenyon's speaker details the onslaught of depression when she was born:

> When I was born, you waited
> behind a pile of linen in the nursery,
> and when we were alone, you lay down
> on top of me, pressing

the bile of desolation into every pore. ("1. From the Nursery,"
1-5)

This description of depression entering her body suggests sexual abuse—uninvited, powerful, forced, and violent. She refers to the rapist as an anti-urge, a mutilator of souls, an unholy ghost. She describes the experience of moving in and out of depression, its arbitrary nature, its unpredictability, again suggesting a type of rape. She writes, "There is nothing I can do / against your coming" ("8. Credo," 12-13). Kenyon concludes this poem by describing the bewilderment when depression lifts, how the speaker can no longer remember what the pain was about: "What hurt me so terribly / all my life until this moment?" ("9. Wood Thrush," 9-10). This clear depiction of how the medical community describes clinical depression is a new subject in poetry and, again, one that declares mental illness cannot and should not be hidden: the subject of a chemical imbalance in the brain is no more shameful than the subject of diabetes, cancer, or any other disease. Clinical depression affects many more women than men, a reality of women's lives that will no longer be hidden.

The desire of women poets to write from the point of view of the experiencer and from inside the moment are the impetus, I believe, of their writing about the subjects discussed above. It seems to me that the same impetus may partly explain their willingness to reexamine traditional beliefs about death and dying. The poetry of Jane Hirshfield and Mary Oliver describes dying and entering the afterlife in a fresh and positive way. Traditionally, readers have been presented with negative images of death such as that of the grim reaper. Poet Dylan Thomas is partly remembered for his poem "Do Not Go Gentle into That Good Night" where he instructs his father "To rage, rage against the dying of the light" (3, 9, 15, 19). While this poem is about Dylan's father going blind, it has come to be understood as a statement about dying. The Church for centuries has taught that Saint Peter stands at the gates of heaven judging who will pass through heaven's gates and who will descend to eternal damnation. Given this traditional view of death, readers are sure to find some relief when introduced to a new mythology about greeting that day.

An entirely new vision of dying is presented by Jane Hirshfield's poem "At the Roosevelt Baths." At the outset the poem gives the appearance of a luxurious and frivolous method of escape, but in fact Hirshfield creates a new mythology for the day of death. She seems to be telling her readers not to be afraid of death because they will be cared for and loved at that important time in their lives. Is this not a fresh and wonderful myth of dying? The speaker in the poem tells the story of a day with several of her friends at the mineral baths where large women armed with thick towels and great white sheets mother them from one step to the next. They run the baths—

> Soon they are doing their math,
> adding, subtracting, swinging cool water into the hot
> with a sweeping of hands;
> they wrap pillows in worn toweling ... (13-16)

Finally the attendants "return softly clucking / and tucking us back into seam- / less white sheeting and sag-bellied cot" (27-28) leaving them to steam. She considers the experience:

> This I trust is the way that
> the angels will be
> on the days of our deaths.
>
> Just this friendly, this homely,
> with just this having-seen-it-all air—
> the smooth and the scabbed, the wrinkled, the lonely,
> the hip-boned and flabbed, all put in their care.
>
> They will wrap
> us in sheets, immerse us
> in bubbling, dark waters,
> they will tell us to nap.
>
> And when we awaken, snap,
> it will be
> into just such a day as today:
> filled with the chittering
>
> of children and thunkety tennis balls,
> always well hit,
> thunkety, thunkety,
> clearing the net. (42-60)

And so ends the poem. Hirshfield has brought her readers through the sensuous experience of a day at the baths to a lovely anticipation of the moment of death and being in the afterlife.

Mary Oliver also presents an alternative point of view about dying in her poem "When Death Comes" by presenting how she wants to think and feel about herself at the end of her life. Oliver's work, like Hirshfield's, gives readers and writers permission to think anew in reconstructing their world-and-life views. While she opens the poem with frightful comparisons of death coming—"like the hungry bear in autumn" (2), "like the measle-pox" (5), "like an iceberg between the shoulder blades"(8)—she continues the poem with a hopeful and energetic view of dying and the afterlife:

> I want to step through the door full of curiosity, wondering:
> what is it going to be like, that cottage of darkness?
>
> And therefore I look upon everything
> as a brotherhood and a sisterhood,
> and I look upon time as no more that an idea,
> and I consider eternity as another possibility, (9-14)

then lists what she finds valuable to her in this life. She concludes the poem anticipating the moment of her death:

> When it's over, I want to say: all my life
> I was a bride married to amazement.
> I was the bridegroom, taking the world into my arms.
>
> When it's over, I don't want to wonder
> if I have made of my life something particular, and real.
> I don't want to find myself sighing and frightened,
> or full of argument.
>
> I don't want to end up simply having visited this world. (21-28)

This poem urges readers to live fully within each moment of their lives and to prepare to enter death with the same fervor.

These women writers, who continuously create their own rules for writing and thereby free themselves to write about new subjects, also choose frequently to use imagery taken from women's traditional work. Thus they suggest that women's work will no longer be hidden, that the motions and machinery of this work are in themselves worth noting and can be useful in clarifying life's intricacies and complexities. Sewing and quilting are only two of the many aspects of women's work that are used as vehicles to process universal truths concerning life and death.

In "I Watched a Snake," Jorie Graham compares a needle moving up and down through a piece of cloth to a snake disappearing and reappearing in the grass. The sewing action becomes a metaphor for the process of integrating the visible and the invisible, death and rebirth: "It took it almost half / an hour to thread / roughly ten feet of lawn" (9-11).

> This must be perfect progress where
> movement appears
>         to be a vanishing, a mending
> of the visible
>         by the invisible—just as we
> stitch the earth,
>         it seems to me, each time
> we die, going
>         back under, coming back up....
> It is the simplest
>         stitch, this going where we must,
> leaving a not
>         unpretty pattern by default. But going
> out of hunger (21-34)

Just as the snake disappears to get sustenance, so must we go down into some dark place removed from rationality and reality to find meaning and identify our values: "Passion is work / that retrieves us, / lost stitches. It makes a pattern of us, / it fastens us / to sturdier stuff / no doubt" (55-60). What is important and interesting about Graham's images taken from women's work is that they are perfect for displaying the huge issue of creating a grounded life for oneself. Graham here marries the domestic image of the sewing needle and its emotional connotation of security and warmth with the passionate search for meaning in life.

In "To a Friend Going Blind," Graham views sewing and its final product as transformative, and so comments on the role of art in this world. Graham focuses on the sensuous quality of choosing fabric for sewing a dress and the pleasure the seamstress feels with her finished product. Here Bruna is teaching the speaker how to sew:

> Saturdays we buy the cloth.
> She takes it in her hands
> like a good idea, feeling
> for texture, grain, the built-in
> limits. It's only as an afterthought she asks
> *and do you think it's beautiful?"* (10-15)

The capstone of this poem is the pleasure Bruna takes in her finished product:

> When Bruna finishes her dress
> it is the shape of what has come
> to rescue her. She puts it on. (35-37)

This character has been rescued and transformed through the process of sewing a dress.

Eavan Boland also suggests that the objects of women's work provide the transforming quality of art in this world. Her poem "In a Bad Light" is about premonitions of war, death, and exile and the need to escape momentarily from these thoughts. Boland asserts the value of women's work by examining a dress sewn by Irish immigrant women and worn in 1860 by a woman on a steamboat bound for New Orleans. Boland thinks about the women who sewed the dress in "oil-lit parlours" (21) and "gas-lit backrooms" (22) "bent over / in a bad light" (25-26) who know they are sewing their "own death in it" (28-29). By sewing the lavish silk dress, the women create beauty in the midst of impending death:

> We dream a woman on a steamboat
> parading in sunshine in a dress we know
> we made. She laughs off rumours of war.
> She turns and traps light on the skirt.
> It is, for that moment, beautiful. (36-40)

Throughout Sandra McPherson's collection of poems entitled *The God of Indeterminacy*, the women's work of quilting is identified with the qualities of art that enrich the human spirit. In the preface to this volume, McPherson states that the book "is about aesthetics, even metaphysics, as manifested in some often unlooked-at corners of culture in America and more distant places.... The reader might find that the center is indeed in the corner or elsewhere, the indeterminate godly place without a name." Here she suggests that the aesthetic and spiritual qualities of women's work, thinking, and understanding may be at the heart and center of culture, and that it has been marginalized and neglected. In other words, what has been the center of attention and considered the truth in the past may not be valid because the truth may reside in what has been ignored, such as the spiritual and cultural evidence found in quilts.

In "Twelve-Bar Quilt," McPherson compares the life-giving sounds of a blues singer and the desire of his audience to hold on to their response with the spiritual quality revealed in a beautiful quilt:

> and the people want to know
>
> where to get it,
>
> ....
>
> how to come by it,
> how to be born,
>
> who to be born.
> The Quilter sews twelve
> wide rivers to immerse in:
>
> just beyond gospel,
> this violent patch-thing
> is the crib quilt for me. (30-31, 35-42)

The quilt feeds the speaker's spirit by offering her a kind of religious rebirth. In "Quilt of Rights" the speaker feels the steady quality of the quilter's work, noticing how deliberately color follows upon color with "No shadings between the frenzied and the cool" (21). McPherson appreciates the design—"For it is not done with moods. / It is given with a right to color" (24-25). The "right to color" is the source of all visual art and quilters have it; McPherson is suggesting that quilters are artists who know design and color and have been overlooked as artists. McPherson continues this theme in "Holy Woman: Pecolia Warner," who made patterns for her quilts by looking at moving objects before putting them together. McPherson implies that Pecolia Warner was able to appropriate the spiritual quality of her environment into the contemplative stitching of the quilt. In "Willa Ette Graham's Infinity Log Cabin Quilt, Oakland, 1987," McPherson suggests that Graham's quilt conveys the power to deal with the ordinary. She then strongly implies, as do Boland and Graham, that the objects of women's work are works of art with transformative qualities.

In "Quilt Top Discovered at the Muskogee Flea Market and Found to Contain Blocks Resembling Certain Designs of Descendants of Maroons in Suriname," McPherson, through the symbolic meaning of colors in Suriname and through the pattern of the stitching, sees the quilt as "a handwriting / of close, irreproachable stitches" through which the quilter "told herself" (25-28). Here, then, McPherson acknowledges the important work women have done in recording history—of themselves and of nations—in nontraditional ways. Not only have their choices of color and design been influenced by rich and ancient cultures, but the quilters themselves have also been recording those cultures and interpreting those histories. She is suggesting that women's work is important, unrecognized for what it is, and thereby hidden.

The subjects and images from women's poetry that I have focused on in this essay in no way represent the whole of women's writing but stand out as noteworthy contributions. Indeed, the writers mentioned above represent only a small fraction of the women poets who have contributed to the ways women poets are shaping world-and-life views, setting forth new subjects, and enriching the poetic vocabulary. Gillian Clarke refers to these influential women who write poems in the powerful opening stanza of "Women's Work":

> Their books come with me, women writers,
> their verses borne through the rooms
> out between the plum trees to the field,
> as an animal will gather things
> a brush, a bone, a shoe,
> for comfort against darkness. (1-6)

The hundreds of women writing poetry today are creating a poetic reality broader and deeper than ever presented before that weaves a context, a safety net, from which others can write.

# Works Cited

Boland, Eavan. *In a Time of Violence*. New York: Norton, 1994.

Cahill, Timothy. "Daring to Live in the Details." *Christian Science Monitor* 24 June 1996: 16+.

Clarke, Gillian. *Five Fields*. Manchester: Carcanet, 1998.

Clifton, Lucille. *The Book of Light*. Port Townsend, Washington: Copper Canyon Press, 1993.

Cofer, Judith Ortiz. "Cold as Heaven." *The Extraordinary Tide: New Poetry by American Women*. Ed. Susan Aizenberg and Erin Belieu. New York: Columbia Univ. Press, 2001.

——. "Photographs of My Father." *The Extraordinary Tide: New Poetry by American Women*. Ed. Susan Aizenberg and Erin Belieu. New York: Columbia Univ. Press, 2001.

Cooper, Jane. "My Mother in Three Acts." *The Extraordinary Tide: New Poetry by American Women*. Ed. Susan Aizenberg and Erin Belieu. New York: Columbia Univ. Press, 2001.

Daniels, Kate. *Four Testimonies: Poems*. Baton Rouge: Louisiana State Univ. Press, 1998.

Dove, Rita. *Mother Love*. New York: Norton, 1995.

Graham, Jorie. "I Watched a Snake." *Erosion*. Princeton: Princeton Univ. Press, 1983.

Hirshfield, Jane. *The October Palace*. New York: HarperCollins, 1994.

Kenyon, Jane. *Constance*. Saint Paul: Graywolf Press, 1993.

Kizer, Carolyn. *Harping On*. Port Townsend, Washington: Copper Canyon Press, 1996.

Kumin, Maxine. *Nurture*. New York: Penguin Books, 1989.

Ladd, Florence. "Daughter of the Outer Banks." *The Women's Review of Books* Dec. 2002: 19.

——. "Ode to My Great Grandmother." *The Women's Review of Books* Dec. 2002: 19.

McCarriston, Linda. *Eva~Mary*. Evanston: Northwestern Univ. Press, 1991.

McPherson, Sandra. *The God of Indeterminacy.* Urbana: Univ. of Illinois Press, 1993.

Mitchell, Susan. *Erotikon: Poems.* New York: Perennial, 2000.

Olds, Sharon. *The Gold Cell.* New York: Knopf, 1987.

Oliver, Mary. *New and Selected Poems.* Boston: Beacon Press, 1992.

Savageau, Cheryl. *Dirt Road Home.* Willlimantic, Connecticut: Curbstone Press, 1995.

Salter, Mary Jo. "Liam." *The Extraordinary Tide: New Poetry by American Women.* Ed. Susan Aizenberg and Erin Belieu. New York: Columbia Univ. Press, 2001.

Sonia Sanchez. *Wounded in the House of a Friend.* Boston: Beacon Press, 1995.

Stone, Ruth. *Ordinary Words.* Ashfield, Massachusetts, 1999.

Thomas, Dylan. "Do Not Go Gentle into That Good Night." *Norton Anthology of Modern Poetry.* Ed. Richard Ellmann and Robert O'Clair. 2$^{nd}$ ed. New York: Norton, 1988.

Wilner, Eleanor. Foreword. *The Extraordinary Tide: New Poetry by American Women.* Ed. Susan Aizenberg and Erin Belieu. New York: Columbia Univ. Press, 2001.

# Women in Philosophy

by Tülin M. Levitas

During my first semester as a full-time faculty member in the philosophy program at Montgomery College, I decided to go to a Women's Studies meeting. Brianne Friel, who had just returned from a leave of absence following the birth of her son, was presiding as coordinator. I thought to myself that it was fitting that a new mother should be presiding at this meeting. During the meeting, I asked Brianne, "Do you have a class in the Women's Studies Program having to do with women philosophers?" She answered, "No, we do not," and in her ever-inviting manner, she asked, "Do you want to create such a class?" At first, my reaction was, "No, not really." Being a brand new full-time faculty member, I was afraid to take on too much, but later, the idea intrigued me.

I was particularly intrigued because neither in my undergraduate nor in my graduate studies had I encountered a female philosopher. The question that arose in my mind was, "Why not?" Was it true that there were no female philosophers? Or was it that philosophy, a male-dominated discipline, excluded female philosophers from its curriculum? Thus, encouraged by Brianne Friel and Matt Schulte, the coordinator of the philosophy program, I decided to investigate. To my great surprise, I discovered that there were a great number of women philosophers who made significant contributions to the field, ranging from antiquity to contemporary times.

We know today that there were prominent women philosophers throughout the ages, but even as recently as the 19th century, some of the best of them did not dare publish their works under their own names. Instead, they had to publish under their male colleagues' names. All of Harriet Taylor's philosophic work was published under John Stuart Mill's name, and Anna Doyle

Wheeler's work, *The Appeal of One Half of the Human Race, Women Against the Pretensions of the Other Half, Men, to Restrain Them in Political and Thence in Civil and Domestic Slavery* (1825), was published under William Thompson's name. Both Mill and Thompson credit Taylor and Wheeler with the content of their works, but nevertheless the publications did not carry their names as their rightful authors. In the 20th century, of course, many women philosophers have entered the discipline and published under their own names. Many are now familiar with the names of Simone de Beauvoir, Charlotte Perkins Gilman, Hannah Arendt, Ayn Rand, and Angela Davis.

What I want to do in this paper, however, is discuss some of the earlier philosophers and the contributions that they have made to the field. I want to introduce the reader to two different women philosophers representing two different periods in the history of philosophy: Aesera the Lucanian, who probably lived around 350 BCE and was considered to be a Pythagorean, and Héloïse, a French philosopher of the 12th century. Both of these philosophers address moral issues. They both emphasize the role that emotions play in formulating moral judgments. Traditional male philosophers had mainly emphasized rationality rather than emotions. Perhaps this is the reason that women have been excluded from the canon of philosophic literature. Yet, we find today that the discipline of philosophy is much enriched by the contributions that these women have made by focusing on the emotions of love, compassion, and connectedness as well as the intellect.

## AESARA, the Lucanian

In the fragmentary remains of Aesara's work, *Book on Human Nature*[1], we see that Aesara addresses the question of whether people need two different kinds of moral philosophy, virtue ethics for the home and a separate theory of justice for society at large. I will argue that Aesara's answer is a resounding "No," for in her view all moral decisions, whether they relate to the individual, the family, or the larger society, should reflect the appropriate proportions of rationality, compassion, and will power. In this way, Aesara lays the groundwork for feminism, for she argues that social justice depends on women raising just individuals in their homes. In her view, therefore, the work that women have traditionally been associated with, i.e., raising children, is every bit as important as the work that men have been associated with outside the home.

In her discussion of morality and justice, Aesara, like Plato, conceives of the soul as having three parts, but, unlike Plato, one of the parts of the soul has to do with emotions such as love and compassion. This emphasis on love and compassion as a necessary condition for moral action constitutes Aesara's important contribution to the history of philosophy. Aesara argues that we can discover the natural and philosophic foundations of all human law through introspection. Her concept of natural law involves the application of moral law in three areas: (1) individual and private morality, (2) the moral foundation of the family, and (3) the morality on which social institutions are based. Aesara maintains, like Plato, that by analyzing the nature of the soul we can understand the nature of law and justice as they apply to the individual, to the family, and to social institutions.

In Platonic fashion, Aesara conceives of the soul as consisting of three parts: the mind, spiritedness, and desire. The mind, which is analogous to the intellect, analyzes ideas and arrives at decisions. Spiritedness, which is analogous to the will, provides the motivations for action. Desire is analogous to positive affective emotions, such as love and compassion. Aesara argues that human nature provides a standard of morality, law, and justice for the individual, the family, and the state. All moral decisions need to show the appropriate proportions of rationality, will-power, and compassion. Aesara also argues that morality, law, and justice need to be rational because they need to consider all relevant ideas, arguments, and principles. Morality, law, and justice are involved in decisions having to do with matters of fact, obligations, and duties. Yet, in order for morality within the individual, rules and discipline in the family, or societal laws to be effective, spiritedness is essential in order for these rules, principles, or laws to function well either as deterrents or as incentives for action. Personal moral principles, family rules and discipline, as well as societal laws all need to also include love either as compassion and kindness towards others or as self-esteem.

In Aesara's view, an individual needs to formulate moral standards for him or herself in such a way that he or she can reasonably follow his or her dictates. Nevertheless, if one falls short of one's own moral standards, then compassion needs to play a role in being self-forgiving and not unduly obsessing about one's own moral short-comings. In the family, compassion also plays a role in that each member's needs ought to be considered and forgiveness ought to be exercised vis-à-vis individual members' shortcomings. Finally, in society, the justice system needs to be compassionate and forgiving as well, taking into account extenuating circumstances and reasons for non-compliance.

Aesara applies her analysis of the soul to the physical body as well. Like the soul, the body also has several parts that have different functions and that work together with different parts of the soul. The mind judges and evaluates the different sensory information that the body receives. Spiritedness again provides the motivation for bodily actions and desire provides the experience of bodily pleasure. According to Aesara, when the different parts of the body function in appropriate proportions to each other, then balance and harmony are achieved in the body. Thus, health and vigor are defined as "the proper proportional interaction of the parts of the body."[2] Disease and debilitation, on the other hand, would be defined as the disproportionate interaction of the bodily functions. This analysis is reminiscent of the Taoist views of health and disease, which were formulated at about the same time in China. In Chinese or Taoist medicine, health is defined in terms of Yin and Yang energy flowing in proper balance. Disease occurs when the energy flow is not in proper balance. So, remedies for disease aim at putting the energy flow in proper balance, whether through diet, exercise, or acupuncture.

According to the Pythagoreans, women had the responsibility to create morality and justice in the home, while men had the responsibility to create justice in the city or the state. As a Pythagorean, Aesara emphasizes the proportionality of the different elements of the soul and the different functions of the body. As we have seen, all moral action, whether it involves the individual, the family, or society at large, needs to reflect the appropriate proportions of rationality, compassion, and will power. So in Aesara's view, so-called "women's work" is morally equivalent to so-called "men's work" because the foundations of justice are the same in the home and in society. Just and harmonious societies must also have just and harmonious homes. Furthermore, social justice depends on women raising just and harmonious individuals in their homes. Thus, in Aesara's view, women cannot be incidental to social justice since they make it possible.

Aesara's moral philosophy is as relevant to us today as it must have been to her own society. Whether we are at home trying to decide how to discipline our children, or at a public debate on whether punishment or rehabilitation is more effective in our system of justice, or in the United Nations Security Council trying to decide whether a war against Iraq is morally justifiable, we need to apply our rationality, motivations, and compassion appropriately and in a balanced manner to the decisions that we make.

## HÉLOÏSE (1100-1163)

Héloïse was a French philosopher whose life was intricately connected to her philosophy. Her life story, particularly her relationship with the renowned philosopher Abelard, has been told and retold numerous times in novels, poems, songs, motion pictures, and most recently in an opera which I was fortunate to see in May, 2001 in Paris. In her lifetime, Héloïse was quite famous for being a bright young woman who had been educated in the Benedictine convent of Argenteuil. She is known to have studied Latin, Greek, Hebrew, philosophy, history, literature, rhetoric, grammar, and aesthetics. She moved in with her mother's uncle Fulbert when she was sixteen years old.

At the same time, Pierre Abelard was a famous philosopher and unordained cleric living in Paris. He and Héloïse met when he agreed to be her tutor and moved in with Canon Fulbert as well. Being Héloïse's teacher, Abelard influenced her philosophic views, yet we see that Héloïse's views are quite distinct from Abelard's, whether they pertain to metaphysics, morality of intent, or disinterested love. Abelard's metaphysics is dualistic: he conceives of a dichotomy between the body and the soul. He views the body as evil, while the soul is good, and he extends this kind of dualistic view to other areas, such as inferior woman and superior man, black flesh and white bones. The conceptual framework of Western metaphysics has been created on these kinds of dichotomies, which have been used to justify racism, sexism, and repression in general when different groups of people have been characterized as the "other." Héloïse, on the other hand, refuses to accept these dualistic views, as becomes evident in her concept of disinterested love and morality of intent. Thus her contribution to the history of philosophy is a more holistic view of human nature and a more responsible concept of love.

Abelard tells of his meeting with Héloïse in his autobiographical work *Historia Calamitatum* (History of My Calamities)[3] by stating that her gift for letters added to her charm and that, therefore, she was well-known all over the country. Soon afterwards, Abelard began making sexual advances toward Héloïse, which she tried to resist by fighting him off physically. He says, "I frequently forced your consent (for after all you were the weaker) by threats and blows"[4] – after threatening her, he beat and raped her. As a result, Héloïse became pregnant, and Abelard tried to persuade her to marry him in order to legitimize the child and protect her reputation. At first, Héloïse refused to marry him so that he could pursue his career and be ordained as a cleric, but ultimately she agreed to marry — a decision she lived to regret. Both Héloïse and her uncle Fulbert promised Abelard to keep the marriage secret so that he could pursue his career. The uncle, however, announced the marriage and Héloïse continued to deny it for Abelard's sake. As a result, Fulbert started mistreating Héloïse, who had moved back to his house. Abelard then ordered Héloïse to return to the convent at Argenteuil and take the veil. Fulbert was furious that the couple denied the marriage yet authenticated the denial by sending Héloïse to become a nun. He hired a number of thugs to castrate Abelard. Since Abelard could no longer consummate his marriage after his castration, he was finally ordained as a priest. Héloïse knew nothing about this until years afterwards.

Héloïse's philosophy is expressed in her *Epistolae*[5] (Letters) and *Problemata*[6] (Problems), both of which were addressed to Abelard once she became acquainted with the contents of his autobiography. We can see in Héloïse's letters that she believed that one's philosophical views had to be applied to the way one lived his or her life. She argued that if one advocated a particular moral philosophy, one needed to live according to it. This view is most readily apparent in her philosophy of love. As Mary Ellen Waithe[7] tells us, Héloïse's concept of love was influenced by Cicero, for whom the most important attribute of true love is the experience of love itself. Héloïse advocates the concept of disinterested love. In her view, true love is completely unselfish and asks for nothing. A person who loves someone loves that person for who he or she is and supports the beloved fully, helping him or her in achieving his or her goals and realizing his or her highest moral potential. It is because of this view that Héloïse resisted Abelard's sexual advances and even his wish to marry her. She believed that giving in to these advances and to his proposal would not help him achieve his goals, even though she was in love with him. She also believed that giving oneself in marriage for economic gain would be demeaning. As she says in her first letter to Abelard,

> ...a woman should realize that if she marries a rich man more readily than a poor one and desires her husband more for his possession than for himself, she is offering herself for sale. Certainly any woman who comes to marry through desires of this kind deserves wages, not gratitude, for clearly her mind is on a man's property, not himself, and she would be ready to prostitute herself to a richer man, if she could.[8]

Héloïse argues that she would rather be Abelard's concubine than marry him for economic gain or prevent him from being ordained as a priest. She says in the same letter,

> God knows I never sought anything in you except yourself: I wanted simply you, nothing of yours. I looked for no marriage bond, no marriage portion, and it was not my own pleasures and wishes I sought to gratify, as you well know, but yours. The name of wife may seem more sacred or more binding, but sweeter for me will always be the word mistress, or, if you will permit me, that of concubine or whore. I believed that the more I humbled myself on your account, the more gratitude I should win from you, and also the less damage I should do to the brightness of your reputation.[9]

For Héloïse, it is through love that one achieves transcendence. She is transformed by her love for Abelard and believes that Abelard is equally transformed by it. For Héloïse, as Dykeman points out, God is possible through love, not the other way around.[10]

For Abelard, on the other hand, human love is just lust, completely different from the love of God. In his view, love ought to be directed towards God only, and to love God one must pray in order to receive his grace. He argues that sexual love is ugly and degrading and that he could not prevent himself from "dirtying himself" as if he were in a pigsty. He craved, he says, obscene pleasures that are derived purely from lust. He is therefore happy to have lost the organ from which his lust emerged. He feels that he has been cleansed rather than deprived. According to him, his castration removed what was only "sordid and worthless."[11]

Héloïse does not agree with Abelard's view of human love. For her, human love is responsible love. Héloïse maintains that people who love each other have certain obligations to each other: not to harm each other and to make each other happy. So, what Héloïse asks of Abelard in her first letter is not the sexual act, which has become impossible as a result of the castration, but rather care, concern, and closeness to her, if only through letters. In Héloïse's concept of love, which is based on mutual responsibility and concern, Abelard's castration becomes irrelevant. Nevertheless, she does not agree with Abelard's view that sexual love is dirty and base. Quite on the contrary, she says,

> The pleasures of love we shared were for me so sweet, they cannot displease me, nor can they be erased from memory; not only what we did, but the places and times in which we did it, along with you yourself, are fixed in my spirit, so that I live it all over again with you and cannot, even in sleep, be at peace.[12]

But Abelard continues to try to persuade Héloïse to forget about him, since by becoming a nun she has become the bride of Christ.

Both Héloïse and Abelard advocate a morality of intent such that the morality of an action is determined by the intention of the action. Abelard defines "sin" as contempt of God and consenting to act on evil desires. Sin does not have to do with having evil desires or acting on those desires, but with the consent of the individual to do so. Thus, he arrives at the absurd conclusion that the action can be immoral without implicating the actor who has performed the action.

Héloïse, on the other hand, while also advocating a morality of intent, does not exactly agree with Abelard. Héloïse argues that it is not so much what is done, but the motivation from which an action is performed, that determines the morality of the action.

So, clearly the intention matters, not simply as a rational consent of the will, as Abelard suggests, but as a motivating force coming from the heart. In this sense, morality also involves activity, specifically the activity of love. In this view, then, what determines the morality of an action is the feeling which motivates the action.

Abelard's actions towards Héloïse were motivated by power, position, and pleasure. He argues that in his actions towards Héloïse, he never consented rationally to rape her or marry her, but that his lust led him to perform these actions. Héloïse, on the other hand, not only did not consent to the sexual acts and the marriage that followed, but her refusal was motivated by her disinterested love for him. As Mary Ellen Waithe states in *A History of Women Philosophers*, "Where she refused marriage out of disinterested friendship, he pursued marriage out of lust. Where she accepted the veil so that he could pursue the ideal, chaste life of a philosopher and cleric, he hid her to avoid social sanction. Where she extended the same selfless love both before and after his castration, his physical desires vanished."[13] Consequently, Abelard's intentions were as immoral as his actions, while her actions, having been motivated by selfless love, maintained their moral worth.

Having lost all interest in Héloïse as a result of his castration, Abelard forbids her to discuss their personal relationship and tells her to discuss with him only matters pertaining to spiritual guidance in her role as abbess of her convent. She then asks him what the rule for her convent should be since the Benedictine rule was written for men only. By raising questions of this nature, Héloïse brings a feministic attitude to her correspondence with Abelard. Given that women are biologically different than men, Héloïse asks that rules suitable for women be formulated for them. She says, "How can women be concerned with tunics and woolen garments worn next to the skin, when the monthly purging of their superfluous humours must avoid such things?"[14] By asking these questions, Héloïse tries to raise Abelard's consciousness about women's particular situation and struggles in the convent. Furthermore, if women could have rules which pertain specifically to their needs, then they would have what men have, i.e., rules which have been formulated specifically for them.

Although Abelard's philosophy has always had a place in the canon of philosophy, it is only in the last decades of the twentieth century that Héloïse has found her place within it, perhaps because she did not assent to a dualistic metaphysics. Yet, we find today that the discipline of philosophy is much enriched by the contributions that women like Héloïse have made to it by adopting a more holistic metaphysics and ethics and by emphasizing compassion, relationships and connectedness as well as rationality.

## Notes

1. Waithe, Mary Ellen, "Late Pythagoreans: Aesara of Lucania, Phyntis of Sparta and Perictione I" in *A History of Women Philosophers, Volume I/600BC-500AD*, edited by Mary Ellen Waithe, Kluwer Academic Publishers, Dordrecht/Boston/London, 1987, pp. 19-26.

2. *Ibid.*, p. 24.

3. Dykeman, Therese Boos, *The Neglected Canon: Nine Women Philosophers First to the Twentieth Century*, Kluwer Academic Publishers, Dordrecht/Boston/London, 1999, p. 40.

4. Waithe, Mary Ellen, "Héloïse" in *A History of Women Philosophers, Volume II/500-1600*, edited by Mary Ellen Waithe, Kluwer Academic Publishers, Dordrecht/Boston/London, 1989, p. 67.

5. *Ibid.*, p.68.

6. *Idem.*

7. *Ibid.*, p. 73.

8. Héloïse, "Letter #1" in *The Neglected Canon: Nine Women Philosophers First to the Twentieth Century*, edited by Therese Boos Dykman, Kluwer Academic Publishers, Dordrecht/Boston/London, 1999, pp. 54-55.

9. *Ibid.*, p. 54.

10. *Ibid.*, p. 46.

11. Nye, Andrea, "A Woman's Thought or a Man's Discipline? The Letters of Abelard and Héloïse" in *Hypatia's Daughters: Fifteen Hundred Years of Women Philosophers*, edited by Linda Lopez McAlister, Indiana University Press, Bloomington and Indianapolis, 1996, p. 31.

12. *Ibid.*, p. 32.

13. Waithe, *op. cit.*, pp. 77-8.

14. Héloïse, "Letter #5" in *The Neglected Canon: Nine Women Philosophers First to the Twentieth Century*, edited by Therese Boos Dykman, Kluwer Academic Publishers, Dordrecht/Boston/London, 1999, p. 66.

## Works Cited

Dykeman, Therese Boos, *The Neglected Canon: Nine Women Philosophers First to the Twentieth Century*, Kluwer Academic Publishers, Dordrecht/Boston/London, 1999.

Nye, Andrea, "A Woman's Thought or a Man's Discipline? The Letters of Abelard and Héloïse" in *Hypatia's Daughters: Fifteen Hundred Years of Women Philosophers*, edited by Linda Lopez McAlister, Indiana University Press, Bloomington and Indianapolis, 1996.

Waithe, Mary Ellen, *A History of Women Philosophers*, Volumes I and II, Kluwer Academic Publishers, Dordrecht/Boston/London, 1989.

## Contributors

*Teresa Bevin* is an educator, author and therapist. Born in Cuba, she emigrated to Spain in 1969, then to the United States in 1972. A graduate of the University of Maryland and George Washington University she is a professor of Spanish and Mental Health at Montgomery College's Takoma Park campus. She conducts seminars on the implications of cultural diversity for counselors and other public service personnel. She is the author of two novels and a forthcoming children's book.


*Kay Bosgraaf* is a professor of English at the Montgomery College's Rockville campus and teaches creative writing of poetry, modern and contemporary poetry as well as a range of other literature and composition courses. She has a Ph.D. in English and Education from University of Tennessee, Knoxville. She has been featured twice as a poet on a cable television show called *Pandora's Box*. In January, 2001, and February, 2003, she received writers' grants for poetry residencies from the Vermont Studio Center. Her most recent book of poetry is entitled *Song of Solidity*.


*Maureen Edwards*, who holds a doctorate in Health Education from the University of Maryland at College Park, with areas of specialization in stress management and gerontology, is a professor of Health at the Rockville campus and serves as program coordinator for both the health education and the gerontology programs. While at the University of Maryland Health Center, she served as Coordinator of the Stress Management Program for the University. In addition, she has worked as a stress management consultant in both the private and public sectors.

*Brianne Friel* has a Ph.D. in the rhetoric of women's literature, focusing on double-voiced discourse in the works of Zora Neale Hurtston. She taught English composition and women's literature for ten years at Montgomery College, where she was director of the Women's Studies Program and host of a women's issues panel discussion TV show. She also has taught rhetoric at the University of Maryland.

*Robert L. Giron*, professor of English, joined the Takoma Park faculty in 1986. He teaches English composition, film and literature, and creative writing. A graduate of Southern Illinois University at Carbondale, he did post graduate work at the University of Michigan at Ann Arbor in comparative literature and studies at the University of Cambridge in England. He was a fellow under a FIPSE grant to incorporate the scholarship of women and minorities into the curriculum in the late 1980s. The African Diaspora has been another of his interests which has led him to study shamanism across cultures. His work has appeared in national journals, including "Gender and African Diaspora Issues in Film" in Community College Humanities Review and CEA-Magazine, "Social Issues in Chicana Poetry of the 1980s." For several years he directed the Takoma Park Honors Program and spearheaded the development of the Takoma Park Scholars Program. In addition, he has written five collections of poetry and is the founder of Gival Press, located in Arlington, Virginia.

*Rita Kranidis* teaches English and women's studies at the Takoma Park campus. She was a Women's Studies and English double major in college and has pursued her interest in women's issues since then. She holds a B.A. from Mount Holyoke College, an M.A. from C.W. Post Center of Long Island University, and a Ph.D. from SUNY at Stony Brook. Her graduate work focused on Victorian Studies and feminist criticism, and she has published in this area extensively. Her current interest is in global women's issues and the role that women play in re-defining cultural norms. Teaching a diverse student population is a dream come true for her.

*Tülin Levitas* was born and raised in Izmir, Turkey. She received all of her higher education in the United States and hold two master degrees; an M. A. from Boston University in philosophy with a historical emphasis and an M.A. from the University of Maryland with an analytic emphasis in philosophy. She has taught in the philosophy program at Montgomery College for the past fourteen years and has been active in the Women's Studies program. She has taught Introduction to Women's Studies and created two Honors courses: Women in Philosophy I and Women in Philosophy II.


*Dianne Ganz Scheper* is professor emerita at Montgomery College, where she taught literature and composition, and, for a decade, directed the College's Honors Program. She holds a Ph.D. in religious studies from The Catholic University of America, with an emphasis on religion and literature. Her research interests are in American nature writing, women and nature, and the intersections of nature, culture, and religion in contemporary world literatures. Currently she is a faculty associate in interdisciplinary studies at The Johns Hopkins School of Professional Studies and adjunct professor of literary studies at the Community College of Baltimore County.

# Permissions

*Introduction.* Reprinted by permission of Brianne Friel. Copyright © 2005 by Brianne Friel.

*Global Women's Studies: An Essay in Three Life-Stories.* Reprinted by permission of Rita S. Kranidis. Copyright © 2005 by Rita S. Kranidis.

*Cuban Women: Betrayed in Revolution.* Reprinted by permission of Teresa Bevin. Copyright © 2005 by Teresa Bevin.

*Women's Work: Environmental Activism in India and Kenya.* Reprinted by permission of Dianne Ganz Scheper. Copyright © 2005 by Dianne Ganz Scheper.

*Where Are the Women in Women's Health?* Reprinted by permission of Maureen Edwards. Copyright © 2005 by Maureen Edwards.

*Caught Between Homophobia and Peer Pressure: A Classroom Experiment.* Reprinted by permission of Teresa Bevin. Copyright © 2005 by Teresa Bevin.

*Women in Front of and Behind the Camera.* Reprinted by permission of Robert L. Giron. Copyright © 2005 by Robert L. Giron.

Their Eyes Were Watching God *and the Quest for Woman's Voice.* Reprinted by permission of Brianne Friel. Copyright © 2005 by Brianne Friel.

*Giving Voice to the Unspeakable: Contemporary Poems by Women.* Reprinted by permission of Kay Bosgraaf. Copyright © 2005 by Kay Bosgraaf.

*Women in Philosophy.* Reprinted by permission of Tülin M. Levitas. Copyright © 2005 by Tülin M. Levitas.

# Books Available from Gival Press

*A Change of Heart* by David Garrett Izzo
1st edition, ISBN 1-928589-18-9, $20.00

A historical novel about Aldous Huxley and his circle "astonishingly alive and accurate."
— Roger Lathbury, George Mason University

*An Interdisciplinary Introduction to Women's Studies*
Edited by Brianne Friel & Robert L. Giron
1ˢᵗ edition, ISBN 1-928589-29-4, $25.00

A succinct collection of articles written for the college student of women's studies covering a variety of disciplines from politics to philosophy.

*Bones Washed With Wine: Flint Shards from Sussex and Bliss* by Jeff Mann
1st edition, ISBN 1-928589-14-6, $15.00

A special collection of lyric intensity, including the 1999 Gival Press Poetry Award winning collection. Jeff Mann is "a poet to treasure both for the wealth of his language and the generosity of his spirit."
— Edward Falco, author of *Acid*

*Canciones para sola cuerda / Songs for a Single String* by Jesús Gardea;
English translation by Robert L. Giron
1st edition, ISBN 1-928589-09-X, $15.00

A moving collection of love poems, with echoes of *Neruda à la Mexicana* as Gardea writes about the primeval quest for the perfect woman. "The free verse...evokes the quality and forms of cante hondo, emphasizing the emotional interplay of human voice and guitar."
— Elizabeth Huergo, Montgomery College

*Dead Time / Tiempo muerto* by Carlos Rubio
1st edition, ISBN 1-928589-17-0, $21.00

Winner of the Silver Award for Translation - 2003 *ForeWord Magazine*'s Book of the Year. This bilingual (English/Spanish) novel is "an unusual tale of love, hate, passion and revenge."
— Karen Sealy, author of *The Eighth House*

*Dervish* by Gerard Wozek
1st edition, ISBN 1-928589-11-1, $15.00

Winner of the 2000 Gival Press Poetry Award. This rich whirl of the dervish traverses a grand expanse from bars to crazy dreams to fruition of desire. "By Jove, these poems shimmer."
— Gerry Gomez Pearlberg, author of *Mr. Bluebird*

*Dreams and Other Ailments / Sueños y otros achaques* by Teresa Bevin
1st edition, ISBN 1-928589-13-8, $21.00

Winner of the Bronze Award for Translation – 2001 *ForeWord Magazine*'s Book of the Year. A wonderful array of short stories about the fantasy of life and tragedy but filled with humor and hope. "*Dreams and Other Ailments* will lift your spirits."
— Lynne Greeley, The University of Vermont

*The Gay Herman Melville Reader* by Ken Schellenberg
1st edition, ISBN 1-928589-19-7, $16.00

> A superb selection of Melville's work. "Here in one anthology are the selections from which a serious argument can be made by both readers and scholars that a subtext exists that can be seen as homoerotic."
> — David Garrett Izzo, author of *Christopher Isherwood: His Era, His Gang, and the Legacy of the Truly Strong Man*

*Let Orpheus Take Your Hand* by George Klawitter
1st edition, ISBN 1-928589-16-2, $15.00

> Winner of the 2001 Gival Press Poetry Award. A thought provoking work that mixes the spiritual with stealthy desire, with Orpheus leading us out of the pit. "These poems present deliciously sly metaphors of the erotic life that keep one reading on, and chuckling with pleasure."
> — Edward Field, author of *Stand Up, Friend, With Me*

*Literatures of the African Diaspora* by Yemi D. Ogunyemi
1st edition, ISBN 1-928589-22-7, $20.00

> An important study of the influences in literatures of the world. "It, indeed, proves that African literatures are, without mincing words, a fountainhead of literary divergence."
> —Joshua 'Kunle Awosan, University of Massachusetts Dartmouth.

*Metamorphosis of the Serpent God* by Robert L. Giron
1st edition, ISBN 1-928589-07-3, $12.00

> "Robert Giron's biographical poetry embraces the past and the present, ethnic and sexual identity, themes both mythical and personal."
> — *The Midwest Book Review*

*Middlebrow Annoyances: American Drama in the 21st Century* by Myles Weber
1st edition, ISBN 1-928589-20-0, $20.00

> "Weber's intelligence and integrity are unsurpassed by anyone writing about the American theatre today..."
> — John W. Crowley, The University of Alabama at Tuscaloosa

*The Nature Sonnets* by Jill Williams
1st edition, ISBN 1-928589-10-3, $8.95

> An innovative collection of sonnets that speaks to the cycle of nature and life, crafted with wit and clarity. "Refreshing and pleasing."
> — Miles David Moore, author of *The Bears of Paris*

*Prosody in England and Elsewhere: A Comparative Approach* by Leonardo Malcovati
1st edition, ISBN 1-928589-26-X, $16.00

> "To write about the structure of poetry for a non-specialist audience takes a brave author. To do so in a way that is readable, in fact enjoyable, without sacrificing scholarly standards takes an accomplished author."
> —Frank Anshen, State University of New York

*The Smoke Week: Sept. 11-21, 2001* by Ellis Avery
1st edition, ISBN 1-928589-24-3, $15.00

*Writer's Notes Magazine* 2004 Book Award—Notable for Culture.
Winner of the Ohioana Library Walter Rumsey Marvin Award
"Here is Witness. Here is Testimony."
— Maxine Hong Kingston, author of *The Fifth Book of Peace*

*Songs for the Spirit* by Robert L. Giron
1st edition, ISBN 1-928589-08-1, $16.95

This humanist psalter reflects a vision of the new millennium, one that speaks to readers regardless of their spiritual inclination. "This is an extraordinary book."
— John Shelby Spong, author of *Why Christianity Must Change or Die: A Bishop Speaks to Believers in Exile*

*Sweet to Burn* by Beverly Burch
1st edition, ISBN 1-928589-23-5, $15.00

Winner of the 2003 Gival Press Poetry Award
"Novelistic in scope, but packing the emotional intensity of lyric poetry..."
— Eloise Klein Healy, author of *Passing*

*Tickets to a Closing Play* by Janet I. Buck
1st edition, ISBN 1-928589-25-1, $15.00

Winner of the 2002 Gival Press Poetry Award
"...this rich and vibrant collection of poetry [is] not only serious and insightful, but sheer delight to read."
— Jane Butkin Roth, editor, *We Used to Be Wives: Divorce Unveiled Through Poetry*

*Wrestling with Wood* by Robert L. Giron
3rd edition, ISBN 1-928589-05-7, $5.95

A chapbook of impressionist moods and feelings of a long-term relationship which ended in a tragic death. "Nuggets of truth and beauty sprout within our souls."
— Teresa Bevin, author of *Havana Split*

## Books for Children

*Barnyard Buddies I* by Pamela Brown; illustrations by Annie H. Hutchins
1st edition, ISBN 1-928589-15-4, $16.00

Thirteen stories filled with a cast of creative creatures both engaging and educational. "These stories in this series are delightful. They are wise little fables, and I found them fabulous."
— Robert Morgan, author of *This Rock* and *Gap Creek*

*Barnyard Buddies II* by Pamela Brown; illustrations by Annie H. Hutchins
1st edition, ISBN 1-928589-21-9, $16.00

"Children's literature which emphasizes good character development is a welcome addition to educators' as well as parents' resources."
— Susan McCravy, elementary school teacher

For Book Orders Only, Call: 877.727.5764
Or Write : Gival Press, LLC / PO Box 3812 / Arlington, VA 22203
Visit: www.givalpress.com